D0955337

ROT, RIOT, AND REBELLION

ROT, RIOT, AND REBELLION

Mr. Jefferson's Struggle
to Save the University
That Changed America

REX BOWMAN *and* CARLOS SANTOS

University of Virginia Press   *London and Charlottesville*

University of Virginia Press
© 2013 by the Rector and Visitors of the University of Virginia
All rights reserved
Printed in the United States of America on acid-free paper

First published 2013

3 5 7 9 8 6 4 2

LIBRARY OF CONGRESS CATALOGING-IN-PUBLICATION DATA
Bowman, Rex.
  Rot, riot, and rebellion : Mr. Jefferson's struggle to save the university that
changed America / Rex Bowman and Carlos Santos.
    pages   cm
  Includes bibliographical references and index.
  ISBN 978-0-8139-3470-9 (cloth : alk. paper)—ISBN 978-0-8139-3471-6 (e-book)
  1. University of Virginia—History. 2. Jefferson, Thomas, 1743-1826—Influence.
3. Universities and colleges—United States—History.   I. Title.
  LD5678.B68 2013
  378.009755'481—dc23
                                                                    2012049804

To our families

B. J. Hendrickson Santos, Michael, Katie, Sarah, and Jaiden

and Jennifer Bowman, Cody, and Carey

The Southerner asks concerning any man, "How does he fight?"
The Northerner asks, "What can he do?"
—Ralph Waldo Emerson

CONTENTS

Illustrations follow page 72

Introduction

The University of Virginia is one of the nation's top public universities. Its alumni, known as the Wahoos, would say it's not one of the best— it's *the* best. The school annually tops collegiate rankings, routinely produces captains of industry, and turns out top-notch scholars the way lesser schools crank out football champions. The university's endowment stands at an incredible $5 billion. Nearly two centuries after its creation, its success now seems preordained—its founder, after all, was the American genius Thomas Jefferson. But his school—a radical experiment that would lay the groundwork for fundamental and dramatic changes in American higher education—almost failed.

During the university's first twenty years, its leaders struggled to keep it open. The school was often broke, and Jefferson's enemies, crouched and ready to pounce, constantly looked for reasons to close its doors. The university, his critics said, was godless, catered to the rich, and was built in the wrong place—"in a poor old turned out field" in backwater Charlottesville. And most important, its first students, though few in number, turned Jefferson's vision of an orderly "academical village" into an early incarnation of an ugly Wild West town.

Although some students came to learn, many came to lark and laze. These students of the first two decades, often the spoiled, self-indulgent scions of southern plantation owners, sometimes the sons of prosperous merchants, led a life of dissipation. With a sense of honor easily bruised, they were reflexively violent. The wrong word, the wrong look could easily lead to a scuffle, if not a duel. Calling a young man a "puppy"—innocuous by today's standards—could get one shot. Cursing in the presence of a lady could lead to a whipping. The students brandished guns freely, sometimes shooting in the air, sometimes at each other. They secreted dirks and daggers and, with little to no thought and even less hesitation, stabbed each other. They pummeled, kicked, bit, and gouged each other. They brawled with town merchants, they scuffled with the local wagoners. They cheated at cards for money. They robbed graves. They gambled on cockfights. They beat slaves. They cursed each other, townsfolk, and professors. They vandalized property (even taking a hatchet to the front doors of the Rotunda, the university's signature building) and mutilated cows. They drank and drank and drank. And rioted.

Their wrongdoing would have kept a modern city police department busy, but this was the mayhem of a tiny student body that averaged fewer than two hundred students per year. (In its first year, 1825, the school enrolled 125 students; in the following years, 177, 128, 131, 120, 133, 133, 140, 158; and in the tenth year, 205.) Modern readers can't fully appreciate early students' behavior and the agony it caused Jefferson because even eyewitness accounts—couched in the polite language of the era—provide only a glimpse of the university's raw beginnings. As the historian J. H. Powell noted, "The historian can never construct a record of events. All he can do is construct a record of records."[1] Still, the depth of the students' depravity astonishes us today.

Professors occasionally armed themselves, and with good reason. One professor was horsewhipped. Others were attacked in their classrooms. One was a target of a bomb—twice. Student William H. Hall of Harper's Ferry, Virginia, surreptitiously set an ink bottle packed with gunpowder on Professor George Tucker's windowsill. Hall had corked the bottle, inserted a hollow quill through the cork, and run a fuse through the quill to the gunpowder. He lit it, but it failed to explode. His second bomb also failed to go off. Hall was expelled. His perplexed father wrote and demanded further investigation, noting in his son's defense that the boy had just been expelled from Harvard College for the same offense. "It seems extremely improbable that he should have so soon repeated" a bombing attempt, the father argued with logic muddled by love.[2]

But such vicious acts were not uncommon in the school's early years, and sometimes student behavior escalated beyond viciousness to full-blown rioting. The school endured at least a half dozen riots in its first twenty years. Hundreds of militiamen were called in to quell one of them. In a strange twist, the students' celebration on the anniversary of one riot led to the murder of a professor. The disturbances damaged the school's reputation, threatened the university's future, and jeopardized critical financial support from the state legislature.

There was also the usual schoolboy mischief. Students "smoked" each other out of their rooms, rolled flaming tar barrels between the dormitories, sang filthy songs learned from plantation slaves, and pounded drums after midnight to annoy and awaken tired professors and fellow students. In one instance, the rowdy revelers explained the noise was "only for the purpose of serenading."[3] The professors, however, already on edge from the casual violence, had little patience for even harmless tomfoolery.

Violence in the United States' universities was all too common during the republic's early years. In schools both of the North and the South, students looked for excuses to smash furniture, break glass, and resist authority. Students often seemed glad to escalate confrontations with professors into riots. What made the mayhem at the University of Virginia unique was the stakes; the school was new and experimental, unsure of the public's support and uncertain of its own future. No powerful church denomination backed the university, no well-connected alumni group stood ready to come to its defense. Its leaders understood that student drunkenness, violence, and rebellion could result in the university's ruin, so they acted as if, in the public's mind, the school were on a probationary period, a period during which Virginia's leaders would decide if they would continue to support this new kind of university on the American landscape.

For Jefferson's university was a bold experiment, a break from centuries of educational tradition. At America's other colleges and universities, modeled primarily on England's Cambridge and Oxford, Greek and Latin formed the heart of the curriculum taught to all students. (The languages were essential to the three gentlemanly professions of law, medicine, and the clergy.) Jefferson, at heart a futurist, dared to give students other options, creating an elective system in which they could choose what to learn. Also, in a bold contrast to other schools—a contrast that would ensure attacks by the powerful religious establishment of the day—Jefferson's institution was secular, free of religious control, with no particular theological doctrine forced on students. Unlike every other university, Jefferson's school did not have a chapel on campus. And finally, the great democrat wanted his students to govern themselves as much as possible, an ambition few other schools would even consider. He believed fear, used as a motivator, was corrosive, that "human character is susceptible to other incitements to correct conduct, more worthy of employ, and of better effect."[4] Pride, ambition, and morality would lead students to behave, Jefferson believed. Students' honor would make strict rules unnecessary. In the words of one of the school's early historians, it was "the University of Adolescent Freedom which Jefferson had in view, and not the College of Juvenile Discipline."[5]

But while Jefferson's elective scheme, utilitarian curriculum, and secularization spread to universities across the nation and are the hallmarks of today's system of public higher education, his lofty philosophy of student self-government nearly destroyed his young university. Jefferson had expected his inaugural class to be mature young men from Virginia and the southern states, students upright and eager to learn. Instead, many of the students, away from their parents' watchful eyes, went wild, more intent on entertainment than education. The students, perhaps more accustomed to giving orders than taking them, bristled at even the modest regulations Jefferson had imposed. Another obstacle was the clash of culture between students and the professors Jefferson had imported from Europe. The professors, lured by Jefferson with promises of top pay at a top-notch university filled with students thirsty for knowledge, were shocked by many of the students' indifference to learning, as well as their recklessness, disrespect, and violence. These students were more violent than anyone—especially Jefferson and his faculty of genteel scholars—could ever have envisioned.

The following years became a grinding struggle to rein in the students and to maintain public support and the money that meant. Tough rules were laid down. In reaction, students rebelled. The rules changed.

The students rebelled again. The university became a morass of punishments, reprisals, unhappy compromises, petty infractions, and petty complaints among students, professors, and the governing board. The already charged atmosphere was made even more explosive by a spectacularly touchy sense of honor the students carried with them at all times.

As early as its first year of existence, Jefferson's school crashed headlong into the culture of honor. But what was honor exactly? Various authors have penned books about the nebulous and complex concept that has become almost an alien notion to modern society. In the nineteenth century, however, the code of honor was the established set of rules under which men in the upper class—in the northern as well as in the southern states—functioned. Honor defined appropriate conduct and established rituals to resolve conflicts. A man without honor—a man who did not understand or follow the code—was unlikely to gain admittance to the ranks of the elite.

"Honor was the core of a man's identity, his sense of self, his manhood," sums up Joanne B. Freeman in her landmark book, *Affairs of Honor: National Politics in the New Republic*. "A man without honor was no man at all. Honor was also entirely other-directed, determined before the eyes of the world; it did not exist unless bestowed by others. Indeed, a man of honor was defined by the respect he received in public. Imagine, then, the impact of public disrespect. It struck at a man's honor and reduced him as a man."[6]

Lacking the bloodlines of Europe's aristocracy and nobility, an American gentleman relied in part on his reputation to assert his position in the ruling class. Honor increased a man's reputation, enhancing his chances of becoming a leader. "Honor was reputation with a moral dimension and an elite cast," wrote Freeman. "A man of good reputation was respected and esteemed; a man of honor had an exalted reputation that encompassed qualities like bravery, self-command, and integrity— the core requirements for leadership."[7]

The code restrained behavior; it was meant to prevent and resolve conflicts. Men were careful not to offend each other's honor unless they were willing to settle a dispute with violence. While much of the stu-

dent misbehavior at the University of Virginia did not revolve around
honor but was simply the kind of rebellion found at other colleges, some
of Jefferson's students repeatedly used the code not as a restraint but as a
license for violence. Then they used the code of honor to shield wrong-
doers—the code, at least in their interpretation, forbade them from in-
forming on each other.

Abetted by their youth and a steady abuse of alcohol, some students
reached for reasons to insult and to be insulted, in order to invoke the
code. Further complicating matters, the vast majority of students were
from Virginia and southern states that shared a similar culture, a culture
in which disputes involving honor frequently led to fisticuffs, sword-
play, and pistol shots. As Freeman conceded, "There were regional
variants of this code as well. Southerners were quicker to duel than
northerners, who withstood the harsher insults but had their own breaking point."[8]

As Bertram Wyatt-Brown, a noted scholar of the honor culture, puts
it: "Few Yankees would feel compelled to settle ideological differences
on a dueling field."[9] Southerners were different. The willingness to fight
and die found its purest form in the duel. In the southern states, duels
between white gentlemen meant not only shooting at each other but also
wielding knives and gouging eyes. In the Savannah area alone, between
1800 and 1840, a total of sixty-three duels were fought, according to one
newspaper editor's tally. Another observer declared that three or four
duels were fought daily in New Orleans. In Mississippi in the 1840s,
duels were "as plenty as blackberries."[10]

The student body at the University of Virginia in its earliest years
was made up almost entirely of young men who grew up below the
Mason-Dixon Line. "The great object of our aim from the beginning
has been to make the establishment the most eminent in the United
States, in order to draw to it the youth of every State, but especially of
the south and west," Jefferson wrote to his great ally Joseph C. Cabell
on December 28, 1822.[11] As Jefferson had noted in an earlier letter on
January 25 of that year, his university would "relieve" southern fathers from sending their sons "to the Northern universities," where,
Jefferson feared, they would pick up political views inimical to southern
interests.[12]

In the first year, 87 percent of the students were Virginians, and almost all the remaining students came from other southern states, according to school records. (The inaugural class featured a single student from the North, a Pennsylvanian, and one student from Great Britain.) Nearly ten years later, the 1834–1835 class of 205 students included no one from the North. Ten years later still, the class of 1844–1845 had 194 students, 2 of whom hailed from northern states—from Massachusetts and Connecticut.

University of Virginia doctoral student Charles Coleman Wall Jr., writing a dissertation years later, calculated that 72 percent of students between 1825 and 1842 were Virginians. Using tax records, he also concluded that the vast majority of students were the sons of "wealthy or well-to-do planters, or of prosperous professional men or merchants living in the cities. The students were the south's upper class."[13] Yet according to school records, northerners virtually shunned Jefferson's school during its first twenty years.

White southern men carried their well-defined sense of honor with them wherever they went, including northern colleges. Harvard graduate Ralph Waldo Emerson, an astute observer of societal conventions, called the southerners he met "bladders of conceit." He summed up the regional differences between southerners and northerners this way: "The Southerner asks concerning any man, 'How does he fight?' The Northerner asks, 'What can he do?'"[14]

To Charlottesville and the university precincts (today called the Grounds), students brought this mind-set. Students stalked the Lawn, ready to fight, eager to prove themselves men of the ruling class, men of honor.

"Acts of Great Extravagance"

On March 19, 1839, Professor Gessner Harrison, a mild-mannered scholar generally liked by the young men who attended his classes at the University of Virginia, strolled out of his lecture hall in the school's stately Rotunda unaware that two students had come looking for him. They were both angry. And armed. William Binford and Thomas Russell had been ordered off the university grounds a month earlier for "gross violations" of school rules. Binford, from outside Richmond, had been suspended until the end of the session. Russell, a Yorktown native, had been dismissed altogether. Harrison, serving as the chairman of the faculty despite his youth, had ordered the two out of the university with the cutting remark that they had disgraced themselves. Now the two had returned on this winter day to avenge this slight to their honor.

They caught up to the professor of Latin and Greek not far from his classroom. Immediately, the two young men demanded that Harrison retract his statement (a standard request among gentlemen looking to satisfy their sense of wounded honor). Harrison, a native of Harrisonburg, Virginia, who was intimately familiar with the gentry's code of conduct and the ease with which young gentlemen could be offended, declined, stating, according to one student's account, "that when he took a stand it was very hard to move him."[1] The powerfully built Binford then asked the professor if he would fight back if struck. A crowd of up to a hundred students had by now gathered around to watch. When Harrison replied that his religious views prevented him from exchanging blows, an enraged Binford seized him by the collar, shook him, and called him a coward. Suddenly, Russell pulled out a horsewhip—its leather hard enough to sting a horse's hide and rip a man's flesh—and slashed Harrison several times as Binford held him. The crowd of students, who had done nothing up to now to defend their professor, were roused to action. Horsewhipping itself was a violent though acceptable form of insult under the gentleman's code of honor, but whipping someone who was being pinned down was far beyond the limits of gentlemanly conduct. The students freed Harrison from his attackers.

But, once loose from Binford's grip, the humiliated professor told the two men they had again disgraced themselves. Infuriated, the two renewed the horsewhipping. "Neither of them pretended that I had done him any injury," Harrison wrote later that day, his handwriting steady despite the beating, in the journal he kept as part of his duties as faculty chairman.[2]

Satisfied that they had punished Harrison sufficiently, Binford and Russell released him, mounted their horses, and galloped off down the Lynchburg road, "giving out that they were going to Mississippi."[3] After witnessing the assault on their professor, the other students made no move to capture them. But university officials rushed to obtain a warrant for their arrest and handed it to the local sheriff, and the school's proctor promised him a one-hundred-dollar reward if he could capture the fugitives before they left Albemarle County, the rolling countryside that surrounded the fledgling university.

Harrison justified the expense as necessary, given the "assassinlike character of the outrage."[4] Binford and Russell, though, outraced their pursuers and escaped to Nelson County, southwest of Albemarle and beyond the local sheriff's jurisdiction. Unluckily for the fugitives, they owed money to a member of the sheriff's posse, a tailor. He refused to let the two men get away without paying their debts. Continuing the pursuit, the tailor caught up to them at the Nelson County courthouse and had their horses and baggage seized. The two men straggled back to Charlottesville on foot and lay low but bolted anew when the university obtained a second warrant for their arrest. The sheriff was nowhere to be found, so the school turned to a shopkeeper named Bailey for help. Though a merchant, Bailey had once been a constable, and the university reiterated its willingness to pay a one-hundred-dollar reward. So Bailey assembled his own posse and set out in pursuit. He caught up with the two students in Fluvanna County, east of Albemarle on the road to Richmond. The desperadoes did not submit without a fight, and during the shootout Russell was "dangerously wounded" by a shot from one of the posse members. Binford was brought to the jail in Charlottesville.[5]

By now, though, student sentiment had turned. Where before they had seen Harrison as the victim of an ungentlemanly act, they now saw Binford and Russell as two classmates being unfairly hounded by a repressive authority. A mob of up to 150 students, the greater part of the student body, gathered around the jail and threatened to break in and rescue their classmate, "all seemingly ready to commit acts of great extravagance," Harrison noted in his journal.

Harrison and the proctor went to the courthouse to attend Binford's trial (the wheels of justice turned considerably faster in the nineteenth century), only to find a local Baptist preacher, the Reverend Tinsley, pleading for leniency. Tinsley said Binford had expressed great and sincere regret. As the mob of students continued to threaten a violent breakout unless Binford was freed, Harrison consulted with "a number of respectable gentlemen of Charlottesville," who told him university officials should simply drop the charges. No one, the gentlemen advised, would think that the threatening mob of students had intimidated the university into capitulating. "Finding it a question of great doubt whether the University would be benefitted by prosecuting the matter further, and considering the danger that it might rather be injured by such a course, the prosecution under the warrant was dropped after Binford had made a written apology, and a promise had been given by the students gathered in Charlottesville, to disperse quietly," Harrison wrote in the journal. This course, he added, "seemed under the circumstances altogether preferable."

The mob of students, though, did not disperse quietly despite their promise. Some of them attacked Bailey's shop, doing as much damage as they could. Tired at last of the student unrest, the citizens of Charlottesville picked up their pistols and rifles and forcibly drove the students back to their dormitories. Binford was released, and Russell disappeared.

At the university, the students quieted down, at least for the moment. But soon, violence would erupt once more, as it had so many times in the fifteen years since the university's founding. And this time, as people wondered out loud if Thomas Jefferson's university was worth the bother, a professor would lie dead.

The Ugly Beginning

Among his many talents, Thomas Jefferson knew how to make enemies. Long before his profile was stamped on the nickel and long before his bust was carved into a South Dakota mountainside—in short, long before his image became a symbol of the American democratic impulse—the sage of Monticello had adversaries, and they were legion. Many citizens of the new nation did not warm to the laconic Jefferson the way they did to his equally taciturn fellow Virginian George Washington. Upon the old general they virtually conferred Old Testament status. Meanwhile, the studious Jefferson, with his hair the color of hellfire and his mind constantly at war with tradition, became a lightning rod for critics.

In his time, Jefferson was publicly accused of cheating his legal clients, detesting the Constitution, denying Noah's flood, and turning his slave plantation into a "Congo Harem" by bedding house slave Sally Hemings, one of the hundreds of slaves Jefferson owned.[1] Weary of his world-shaking, "leveling" ways,[2] his conservative foes opined that the whippet-thin intellectual should stick to pinning insects and tinkering with swivel chairs. When he won election to the presidency in 1800, tradition holds, the women of New England hid their Bibles in their wells, convinced that Jefferson's atheistic minions would snatch them up and cast them on bonfires.[3] Even when he doubled the size of the nation with the Louisiana Purchase, Jefferson's detractors were unimpressed: thanks to an unabating anti-Jeffersonian sentiment, none of the states formed from the newly purchased land were named after the president.

And, in a criticism that wounded him far more deeply than any of the crackpot assertions about his religious beliefs, political opponents accused him of running a con game to get the money he needed to build a university in Virginia. "There are fanatics both in religion and politics," Jefferson complained to state senator Joseph C. Cabell, "who, without knowing me personally, have long been taught to consider me as a raw head and bloody bones."[4]

Jefferson sowed the seeds of his own unpopularity as a young member of the Virginia legislature. Born in 1743 in Shadwell, Virginia, not far from the dusty trade town of Charlottesville, Jefferson was in his twenties when he won election to the state House of Burgesses in 1768. He was a young radical in the midst of what until then had been an archly conservative lawmaking body. Jefferson's early years in the Williamsburg chamber passed quietly, but in 1776, after he had taken time out to ride to Philadelphia, attend the Continental Congress, and pen the Declaration of Independence (thereby putting the colonies at war and adding the entire British government to his growing list of enemies), he suggested to his fellow legislators that the laws of Virginia needed a thorough overhaul. They were a hodgepodge of ancient British law and turgid legalistic jargon, and furthermore, in Jefferson's view, they enshrined superstition and unnecessarily restricted the freedom of citizens.

So in October 1776, Jefferson offered a bill proposing that the House of Delegates (formerly the House of Burgesses) appoint a committee of five members to reform state laws. His liberal allies backed the plan, and the House appointed Jefferson to the committee. He immediately set about rewriting the laws of Virginia, crafting so many bills that the General Assembly, slowed perhaps by the ongoing Revolutionary War, would need years to discuss and vote on them. By the spring of 1779 Jefferson's committee had written 126 reform bills. Jefferson pushed his colleagues to adopt them, convinced that the revolutionary mood was the best time to make radical changes. "The time for fixing every essential right on a legal basis is while our rulers are honest and ourselves united," Jefferson wrote of his flurry of bill writing. "From the conclusion of this war we shall be going down hill."[5]

The legislature, often descending into rancorous debate, took a decade to ponder Jefferson's reforms. And though some bills—such as the one calling for the eventual emancipation of slaves—were never acted on, others passed, turning the Old Dominion into a testing ground for democratic reform. In accordance with Jefferson's bills, the laws of primogeniture and entail, which restricted who could inherit and own land, were abolished. The capital was rooted up from Williamsburg and moved to the village of Richmond, more central to the state's population. The death penalty, a possibility for petty criminals and horse thieves, was abolished for all crimes except murder and treason. And, importantly, laws compelling financial contributions to support religion were discarded.

Every change had its foe, however. The old aristocracy steamed at the land reforms that made it easier for the common man to hold property. The "Tories" of conservative Williamsburg were shocked to find themselves on the periphery of power as the state capital moved west. When Jefferson was nominated for Speaker of the House in May 1778, the conservatives, led by Benjamin Harrison (whose son, William, would one day become the nation's ninth president), took the opportunity to punish him, sending him to inglorious defeat on a vote of 51 to 23.

The Episcopalians were outraged at the cut in state funding. So powerful were religious leaders, in fact, that they were able to stymie Jefferson's religious reforms for years. Even after the General Assembly abolished mandatory contributions to religion in 1779, it was still a crime to deny the Trinity, and mothers and fathers could lose custody of their children if they did not subscribe to the Episcopal (formerly known as Anglican) creed. But in 1786, even though it was to cost him decades of enmity, Jefferson's "Act for establishing Religious Freedom" became law, separating the church from state control and leaving citizens free to follow their own beliefs without fear of state punishment. The law is one of the three accomplishments Jefferson had carved into his gravesite obelisk. The others are the writing of the Declaration of Independence and the creation of the University of Virginia.

Still, any joy Jefferson felt at displacing the Anglicans from their place of prominence was tempered by the defeat of the bill closest to his heart—the bill for educational reform (titled the "Bill for the More

General Diffusion of Knowledge"). In Jefferson's view, the survival of democracy depended completely upon an educated citizenry: the ignorant could be led astray into any false political doctrine. Therefore it was imperative that citizens be educated at an early age. According to the plan Jefferson submitted to legislators, every child, boy or girl, would have access to a nearby state-supported elementary school. Superior boys would have access to secondary schools. A state library would be established at Richmond at a cost of £2,000 per year. And capping off the entire system, William and Mary College in Williamsburg would be converted from a church-controlled divinity school to a public university, free of religious dominance. Here, professors would emphasize science, mathematics, and modern languages over theology and the ancient languages of the Bible. The plan was radical, an assertion of the state's responsibility for the education of its citizens and a full-frontal assault on the role of religion in higher education in an era when Protestant denominations controlled the nation's colleges, public and private.[6]

The bill died a slow, agonizing death. Plantation owners paid the taxes in Virginia, and they couldn't understand why they should foot the bill to send poor children to school. Without their backing, no bill could pass the General Assembly. Furthermore, debts from the Revolutionary War made Jefferson's expensive educational reform too costly. Legislators, while enthusiastic in theory, refused to support it in practice.

The defeat, while giving Jefferson a clear picture of the conservative mind-set he was up against, also marked the beginning of his nearly half-century-long struggle to establish a modern public university in his home state. Galling to Jefferson, perhaps, was the success the religious groups were having at founding their own schools. While he was making no headway in the General Assembly, the Presbyterians had established Hampden-Sydney College in rural Prince Edward County in 1776, and they had followed that up six years later by creating Liberty Hall, an academy that ultimately would become Washington and Lee University. The Methodists and Baptists, meanwhile, were carrying out their own educational designs. Religious leaders had a head start, but Jefferson refused to give up his plan for a secular university.

In 1779, Jefferson was not only elected governor but appointed to the Board of Visitors of William and Mary, his alma mater. Full of his customary energy, he quickly set about to change the creaky old institution. And here he had temporary success. The school had been founded by the Church of England a century before the Revolution to supply the colony with seminary-trained Gospel ministers, to educate the young "piously" in "good letters and manners," and to spread Christianity "amongst the Western Indians." So said the school's charter.[7] Under Jefferson's influence, the Board of Visitors abolished the two professorships of divinity and "Oriental" languages. In their place, the school established a professorship of law and police, one of modern languages, and another of anatomy, chemistry, and medicine. To the duties of the moral philosophy professor were added the law of nature and nations and the fine arts. But the Episcopal Church still controlled the college, and it resisted change. Other denominations, meanwhile, withheld their support, interpreting Jefferson's involvement in the school as his support for the Episcopal denomination. And finally, the college languished because Williamsburg, as previously noted, was no longer the cultural center of the state—Jefferson had successfully pushed to move the state capital to Richmond.

But William and Mary wasn't Jefferson's only avenue toward creating a modern university. He toyed with a couple of other options. The first involved a Frenchman, Quesnay de Beaurepaire, who served under Jefferson's great friend the marquis de Lafayette during the Revolution. De Beaurepaire, the grandson of Louis XV's physician, was a modernist when it came to education, and he used his connections to France's elite society to enlist backers for a grandiose plan to establish an academy in Richmond modeled on the great French Academy of Science. According to de Beaurepaire's plan, the Richmond academy of arts and sciences would offer classes in anatomy, architecture, astronomy, botany, chemistry, design, engraving, foreign languages, geography, mathematics, mineralogy, natural history, painting, and sculpting.[8] It was a modern curriculum, in short, nothing like that taught in the religious colleges of eighteenth-century America. It even surpassed the modest reforms Jefferson had brought to William and Mary. It was the kind of curriculum Jefferson could endorse.

De Beaurepaire envisioned branches in Baltimore, Philadelphia, and New York, with affiliations with the royal societies of Paris, Brussels, and London. One hundred and seventy-five associates were to help the professors, who would be selected from among the best minds of Europe and America. Jefferson, by now the U.S. minister to France, allowed his name to be associated with the project, and de Beaurepaire raised 60,000 francs and laid the cornerstone in Richmond in May 1786. But Jefferson had decidedly cooled to the project by 1788. He wrote the energetic Frenchman a letter wishing him success but suggesting that his plans were too grand for a nation as impoverished as the fledgling United States.[9] Jefferson's abandonment of the plan was just as well. The coming of the French Revolution put an end to the scheme as funds dried up. De Beaurepaire's academy was never built.

But less than a decade later, Jefferson, now back at Monticello, was once again entertaining a plan to improve higher education in his state. In 1794, reports reached Jefferson that the professors of the University of Geneva could possibly be enticed into migrating en masse. Several had already stated their willingness to come to the United States. A power struggle had put an aristocracy in charge of the Swiss government that was at odds with the school's doctrines, and the professors were looking for a political haven. Jefferson was intrigued by the idea. In one fell swoop, he could bring an entire faculty of brilliant scholars to Virginia and create a university almost overnight. He could do by himself what the state legislature had refused to do.[10]

Jefferson wrote private letters to several trusted members of the legislature, feeling them out about the possibility of bringing the Geneva faculty to Virginia. Their response was disappointing. Universally, they deemed the project too expensive and too grand for a state as small as Virginia. Furthermore, they balked at the thought that Virginia's youth would be educated in a foreign language. No one but Jefferson, it seemed, found the idea worth pursuing.

Jefferson then appealed to George Washington. Washington had previously spoken of creating a national university by selling some stock he owned in the Potomac and James River companies. Jefferson suggested that the Geneva professors could form the nucleus of the school, which could be located just outside the capital—in Virginia. Washington, arguing that his plans for a national university were still in embryonic form, demurred, noting also his distaste for importing a single group of professors.[11]

Jefferson had been defeated on all fronts. Through inaction, the General Assembly had killed his plan for a public university. De Beaurepaire's plan had proved impractical and too expensive. The great Washington himself had refused to support the importation of the Geneva faculty. And as for William and Mary, Jefferson was ready to wash his hands of it. In 1800, he wrote to fellow scientific tinkerer Joseph Priestley that the old college was "just well enough endowed to draw out the miserable existence to which a miserable constitution has doomed it."[12]

Still, Jefferson had not given up hope of establishing a university elsewhere in Virginia. In the same letter to Priestley, he spoke of a university established "on a plan so broad and liberal and modern, as to be worth patronizing with the public support, and be a temptation to the youth of other States to come and drink of the cup of knowledge and fraternize with us."

Whatever plans he entertained, though, would have to be put on hold. First, Jefferson would seek the presidency.

Building a University in Virginia

Americans spent much of 1800 embroiled in one of the first—and possibly still the fiercest—partisan presidential campaigns in the nation's history, and at the center of the political storm that threatened to capsize the ship of state stood Jefferson. The campaign attacks on his character from politicians and preachers alike deepened the Virginian's mistrust of power and reinforced the anticlerical views he would hold for the rest of his life. And those views, in turn, would help him define for himself how a modern university should work.

As the year 1800 opened, Jefferson was serving out his final months as vice president to President John Adams, an awkward circumstance for the two rivals brought about by Jefferson's loss to Adams, by three electoral votes, in the 1796 election. As runner-up, Jefferson assumed the vice presidency, as the Constitution then dictated. While virtually impotent in matters of policy within the Adams administration, Jefferson wielded great political influence as head of the Republican party. Adams, after Washington's death, had emerged as the leader of the Federalists. While the contest between the two parties occasionally seemed like a quarrel between Anglophiles and Francophiles—Federalists wore the black cockades of the British, while Republicans sported the tricolored cockades of the French—the two parties' supporters genuinely hated each other. Each side was convinced that the other's ascendancy would spell the ruin of the fledgling republic. The rematch between the candlestick-thin Jefferson and the teapot-portly Adams promised to be a bloody affair.

To the Republican way of thinking, the Federalists, with their insistence on a strong executive power, were secretly scheming to establish a government controlled by aristocrats or, worse, a king. Further alarming Republicans, Adams had created an army of fifteen thousand men under the command of the brilliant intriguer Alexander Hamilton—and hadn't one of the complaints against George III been that he'd used the colonies as a garrison for a standing army? Giving Republican suspicions even more credence, the Federalist-controlled Congress had passed the Alien and Sedition Acts, which threatened jail time for the president's critics and made it easier for the Adams administration to throw pro-Republican foreigners out of the country.

Adams, according to Republicans, was on his way to becoming a tyrant. The Polish writer Julien Niemcewicz noted in his diary that the Alien bill, "conceived in a truly Turkish spirit, shows to what point the administration attempts to adopt and imitate the arbitrary means of despots."[1] As Adams's presidency wore on, printers and pamphleteers who opposed him were tried, convicted, and jailed. Among them was British émigré Thomas Cooper, who would later figure prominently in Jefferson's plans for a university. Cooper, who like Thomas Paine began his career as an agitator in Britain before bringing his rabble-rousing skills to America, had published a handbill accusing Adams of trying to create a standing army. On trial in Philadelphia before Justice Samuel Chase, Cooper said he knew that England's king was infallible but didn't know the president shared the attribute. Cooper was led off to prison to serve a six-month sentence, exclaiming as he went, "Is it a crime to doubt the capacity of the president?"[2]

To Federalists, the large army and Alien and Sedition Acts were necessary wartime measures. The country was engaged in an undeclared naval war with France, and many of the most conservative Federalists viewed a French invasion as a possibility. Adams and fellow Federalists considered France, where the Jacobins had overthrown the monarchy and church, the most extreme example of the dangers of egalitarianism, and, at home, they viewed the Republicans' sympathy for French democracy as a portent for potential violence in America. Furthermore, some thought it plausible that French agents would be able to recruit

Republicans and immigrants to their banner if they invaded the United States. The Republicans, Jefferson included, had been notoriously easy-going about accounts of French aristocrats being dragged from their carriages and killed.

So a smear campaign against Jefferson—dubbed "the great arch priest of Jacobinism and infidelity"[3]—began in earnest. Timothy Dwight, a leading evangelical minister and president of Yale, labeled Jefferson a tool of French secularism, asking, "For what end shall we be connected with men of whom this is the character and conduct? Is it that our churches may become temples of reason? . . . Is it that we may see the Bible cast into a bonfire? . . . Is it that we may see our wives and daughters the victims of legal prostitution?" This was going on in France, Dwight contended, and Jefferson would bring it to America. Dwight added: "Shall our sons become the disciples of Voltaire . . . or our daughters the concubines of the Illuminati?"[4]

The *Gazette of the United States*, a pro-Federalist newspaper, called Jefferson an "audacious howling Atheist."[5] A month before the election, the newspaper baldly declared that the question before voters was simply "Shall I continue allegiance to GOD—AND A RELIGIOUS PRESIDENT; Or impiously declare for JEFFERSON—AND NO GOD!!!"[6] Critics saw Jefferson's tolerance of the religious views of others as proof that he was an unbeliever, and his opinion that young students in public schools should study history instead of the Bible enraged them. "On account of his disbelief of the Holy Scriptures, and his attempts to discredit them, he ought to be rejected for the Presidency," the Reverend William Linn summarized in one pamphlet.[7] Another sermonizer summed up Jefferson's disqualifications for the presidency by noting simply, "He does not go to church."[8] Jefferson concluded that religious leaders had singled him out for abuse—despite the fact that his religious views differed little from those of other leading statesmen, including Adams—because he had separated church from state in Virginia. Ministers, Jefferson wrote to Benjamin Rush, would be happy to undo the law and reestablish their links to the government. But, he noted hopefully, "The returning good sense of our country threatens abortion to their hopes, and they believe that any portion of power confided to me will be exerted in opposition to their schemes. And they believe rightly; for I have sworn upon the altar of God eternal hostility against every form of tyranny over the mind of man."[9] The final twenty words are carved into the Jefferson Memorial in Washington, DC. So hostile and active were the Federalists that Jefferson worried that their agents in the post office were reading his mail.[10]

In the end, Jefferson won the election and was later reelected. The achievements and failures of his presidency are the subject of numerous other books. What is important to note here is that Jefferson had made enemies not just in Virginia but across the nation and, significantly, among the religious. Their attitude toward the great democrat would play a role in how Jefferson fashioned his university and how he and his successors managed it.

But Jefferson was unable to turn his attention to the problem of education in Virginia until 1814, and only then through a piece of luck. Riding from Monticello into Charlottesville one winter day, the retired president, now in his seventies, was hailed by a gentleman who stepped out of the Stone Tavern. Inside, five men had gathered to discuss their plans to establish a local grammar school, the Albemarle Academy. The men (Jefferson's nephew Peter Carr, John Carr, John Harris, John Nicholas, and John Kelly) had been appointed trustees of the proposed institution eleven years earlier, yet nothing had been done to turn the idea into reality. The man who stepped outside invited Jefferson to join them. Jefferson did, and the gentlemen promptly elected him to the board of trustees.[11] Whether Jefferson knew of the meeting and intentionally set out for the Stone Tavern remains a mystery, but it seems unlikely he would have been unaware of such an important enterprise in his neighborhood.

Ten days later Jefferson was elected to chair a committee to draft regulations for the school. Six months later he was already scheming to turn the small academy into something much more significant. To Peter Carr, president of the board of trustees, he wrote that he had long contemplated an institution "where every branch of science, deemed useful at this day, should be taught in its highest degree."[12] The Albemarle Academy must be a college, Jefferson concluded, where several of the best professors could teach Virginia's young men.

Of course there was no money for such a scheme. So in January 1815, Jefferson turned to his young friend Joseph Cabell, a member of the state senate, to obtain funds for the school, as well as permission to rename it the Central College. Cabell, in the senate since 1810, was the right man for the job. Virginian Chapman Johnson described him as "clever" with a certain "strength of mind" and a "communicative disposition," as well as being "respectable and respected" and "amiable and beloved."[13] Cabell, a handsome man with a strong jaw, aquiline nose, and broad forehead, also had an introverted side and a tendency to drift.

Born December 28, 1778, in the middle of the Revolution on a plantation on the eastern slopes of Virginia's Blue Ridge, Cabell attended Hampden-Sydney College for one year before enrolling at the College of William and Mary. He idled away his days there before returning home, where he read law with his brother William, who would one day be governor. In 1800, Cabell returned to William and Mary, this time vowing to study hard, but once there, he later recalled, "Scarcely a single Ball or Party of pleasure has escaped me."[14] An ardent Republican and the scion of a Republican family, Cabell noted Jefferson's 1800 election to the presidency as a moment of great joy for himself and his classmates. However, Cabell disliked studying the law. "It deserves all the censure that the lazy, the idle, or the industrious have bestowed on it," he wrote. "The labours of Sysiphus or the punishments of the Daniades were not much worse than the incessant and never ending task of pouring over the mouldey records of Law."[15]

Weary of study, the lifelong sufferer of sundry ailments—he was diagnosed with illnesses as diverse as bleeding lungs, malaria, and liver disease—persuaded his family to let him travel to Europe in order to improve not only his education but his health. So from 1803 to 1806 he traveled about England, France, the Netherlands, and Italy, visiting famous universities along the way.

He returned to Virginia in 1806 and married Mary Walker Carter, the stepdaughter of his law professor at William and Mary, Henry St. George Tucker. Cabell also met his Republican hero President Jefferson, who warmed to the young man. In quick succession, Cabell was elected to the House of Delegates and then to the state senate. By the time Jefferson reached out to him for help, Cabell was a seasoned navigator of Richmond's turbulent political waters.[16]

Regarding Jefferson's request for money to build the school, Cabell was optimistic that he could get the job done unless "certain delegates from the lower counties who might have fears for William and Mary" moved to thwart him.[17] Cabell's political instincts were acute: proponents of the Williamsburg college did indeed feel threatened by the rise of a new institution. In the years that followed, every plan Cabell pitched for the Central College met with opposition from the legislators from the coastal "lower counties."

As the General Assembly wrestled with the issue of higher education, talk turned to the establishment of a state university, and new enemies arose. Friends of Hampden-Sydney fought to make sure their school was not slighted. Meanwhile, delegates from the western part of the state—which then included what is today West Virginia—felt any new university should be located west of the Blue Ridge, possibly at Washington College in Lexington.

In February 1816, Cabell was finally able to write that the senate had established the Central College. However, the victory was not complete: the only money available to build the institution was what Jefferson and the other trustees had been able to get their neighbors to pledge. There was no state funding. Still, the bill establishing the college demanded that the governor appoint six powerful men to serve as a board of trustees. Governor Wilson Cary Nicholas chose Jefferson and Cabell, former president James Madison, future president James Monroe, the politician David Watson, and General John Hartwell Cocke.

Jefferson immediately turned his attention to getting the Central College chosen as the new state university, even as legislators from Staunton and Lexington agitated to have the proposed university placed in western Virginia. Jefferson's strategy was simple: he would buy land and begin building the college. With buildings already in place, he and Cabell reasoned, legislators might be more inclined to pick the Central College as the site of the university.

In May 1817, the trustees agreed to buy a tract in Charlottesville from John Perry. Jefferson had wanted to buy a tract farther east, but it was owned by John Kelly. Kelly was one of the original Albemarle Academy trustees and a Federalist—a member of the political party that championed a strong central government. Jefferson, head of the rival Republican party, had ousted Kelly from the board. Not surprisingly, then, Kelly refused to sell his land, saying, "I will see him at the devil before he shall have it at any price."[18] So the board purchased Perry's land, which had once been owned by Monroe. The board also approved Jefferson's plan for an "academical village."[19] The scheme called for "erecting a distinct pavilion or building for each separate professorship, and for arranging these around a square, each pavilion containing a school room and two apartments for the accommodation of the professor, with other reasonable conveniences."[20] Because none of the pledge money had been paid, construction could not begin. Thus Jefferson and the other trustees also decided to embark on a new fund-raising campaign, with Jefferson promising the first $1,000. By January 1818, they had received more than $35,100 in pledges. On October 6, 1817, workers laid the cornerstone of the first pavilion—one of ten meant to serve as professors' homes and lecture rooms. According to an eyewitness account, to President James Monroe went the ceremonial task of laying the school's cornerstone.[21] Construction was under way.

Meanwhile, Jefferson moved ahead with his plans to turn the college into a university. In the legislative session that year, he had Cabell present his entire scheme for an overhaul of the state's education system. The bill called for a state university, leaving it up to the legislature to determine where to put it. Cabell became a whirlwind of activity, pushing the plan under the nose of every legislator he could find. But everywhere he turned, he found obstacles. Still, he wrote to Jefferson that he hoped the ex-president's bill could unite the sundry factions. "I have only this single anxiety in this world," replied Jefferson, on edge for any word regarding the fate of his educational scheme. "It is a bantling of forty years' birth and nursing, and if I can once see it on its legs, I will sing with sincerity and pleasure my *nunc dimittis*."[22]

Ultimately, though, the legislature rejected Jefferson's bold plan, opting instead only to provide for the education of the poor. A disheartened Cabell, whose only success in Richmond had been in finding the best bricklayers to send to Charlottesville to work on the school's pavilions, wrote to Madison to share his bleak assessment of Jefferson's plan to turn Central College into a state university. "This Assembly will do nothing for the Central College," he wrote in February 1818. The delegates west of the Blue Ridge were divided on whether Staunton or Lexington would be the best site, but they had united to oppose Charlottesville. The Presbyterians, meanwhile, were "hostile" to Jefferson's plan, Cabell noted, while Jefferson's old foes, the Federalists, "view it with a malignant eye." Finally, supporters of William and Mary still regarded Central College as "a future rival."[23]

Cabell concluded: "This combination of unfortunate circumstances defeat our expectations and throw us into utter despair of any success with the present Assembly."[24] But for once, Cabell, usually an astute observer of political winds, was wrong. A few days later the senate passed a bill, on a vote of 14–3, calling for a university. The bill provided that the governor and his council should create a commission, with one commissioner per senate district, to meet at Rockfish Gap on August 1, 1818, to select a site for the university.

The legislative approval was more than Cabell and Jefferson had hoped for. Now they only needed the governor to choose commissioners friendly to the Central College and their dream could be realized. Cabell suggested that all available funds should be spent on construction so that, when August rolled around, as much of the Central College as possible would be standing. Cabell also urged Jefferson to serve on the commission, but Jefferson knew he was a lightning rod for criticism and balked. Ultimately, though, Jefferson allowed himself to be persuaded to join the commission.

Cabell and Jefferson's worries that the commission might be stacked against them were unfounded. Governor James Preston, after all, was a Republican. The two dozen men who formed the commission included not only Jefferson and Madison but Cabell's brother, William H. Cabell; Creed Taylor, who had written to Cabell early in 1818 to pledge his support for Central College; Spencer Roane, a Jefferson supporter; William Brockenbrough, a college chum of Cabell's and the banker who had loaned money to fund construction of Central College; and

A. T. Mason and Hugh Holmes, both of whom had given money to the school.[25]

The Rockfish Gap commission met to determine where the new university would be established. The choices were clear: at Central College in Charlottesville, at Washington College in Lexington, or in the city of Staunton. Jefferson arrived with a map and statistics from the 1810 census to show that Charlottesville was at the very center of the state's white population. He also displayed a list of octogenarians living in Albemarle County, a supposed proof of the area's healthy atmosphere. One tale runs that Jefferson carried in addition a cardboard cutout of Virginia with the exact center of the state marked by a dot. Jefferson proved the dot was at the center by balancing the cutout atop a pencil point. The dot, of course, represented Charlottesville. On August 3, the commission voted Central College and Charlottesville as the site for the new university.

In a detailed report to be given to the General Assembly at its upcoming session, the commission adopted Jefferson's architectural plan and recommended ten professorships and a curriculum that would boldly break from the courses taught at other American colleges. The classes included ancient languages, modern languages, physics (then known as natural philosophy), botany and zoology, anatomy and medicine, mathematics, physico-mathematics, government and history, municipal law, and a hodgepodge of topics including grammar, ethics, rhetoric, belles lettres, and fine arts. These classes would form the heart of Jefferson's new educational scheme—an elective system in which students could choose what to learn. Furthermore, Jefferson envisioned a school where students could come and study for as little as a year or as long as they liked, taking whatever courses they desired to satisfy their academic passions. This fresh, democratic approach to higher education would ultimately spread across the nation. Notably, there was no place for a professor of divinity. "A University with sectarian professorships, becomes, of course, a Sectarian Monopoly: with professorships of rival sects, it would be an Arena of Theological Gladiators," Madison later explained.[26] Students who wished to worship, he added, could always attend the nearby churches in Charlottesville. Meanwhile, according to

Jefferson's wishes, the ethics professor would be welcome to lecture on the proofs of God's existence.

The commission's report was the springboard for further far-reaching reforms. Though the report did not spell it out, it allowed Jefferson to ultimately create a school free of religious control. All colleges in America had presidents, and they were almost always trained ministers. Virginia's new school, thanks to Jefferson, would have no church affiliation and no president; professors would serve as chairmen in rotating order. After arranging for boardinghouses and dormitories, the report moved on to student discipline. Jefferson believed that fear was not a proper motivating force for young men, so the commission report recommended that the university's Board of Visitors be allowed to adopt an approach that would exploit students' "pride of character, laudable ambition, and moral dispositions" to curb any excesses.[27] Unlike other universities, Jefferson's school would trust students to behave; the least government would be the best government.

But the battle was not over. The General Assembly still needed to approve the plan, and the western delegates and William and Mary supporters were hard at work to stymie Jefferson's ambition. The western legislators moved for more time, ostensibly to double-check the population figures that Jefferson had used, while the eastern legislators maneuvered to kill any funding.

"I am really fearful for the ultimate fate of the bill," Cabell wrote Jefferson in December 1818. "Should these parties unite on the question on the passage of the bill, it will be lost; and this result is much to be apprehended."[28] Seven days later, on Christmas Eve, the situation had worsened. The opposition, Cabell wrote, "is growing so rapidly, we have just grounds to fear a total failure of the measure."[29]

Cabell swung into action. Convinced that the western legislators would never change their position, he focused all his attention on the legislators east of the Blue Ridge, who outnumbered their western counterparts. Working district by district, he sought to rally the eastern legislators to his side. By early January, Cabell began to feel he had averted disaster.

But in January 1819, a delegate from Rockbridge County, west of the Blue Ridge, moved to strike out of the university bill the section that named Central College as the site of the university. The delegate suggested Washington College instead. A raucous debate followed, with eastern and western delegates pitted against each other. Delegate Briscoe Baldwin of Augusta County made a novel pitch for Staunton, arguing that the healthy atmosphere "conspires to give the finest bloom to our girls."[30] Two days later, the question of whether to scratch out Central College was put to a floor vote. Cabell, tense with anxiety, could not bear to watch. When the smoke cleared, a vote of 114–69 kept Central College as the designated site. Baldwin, the main proponent for Staunton, now urged reconciliation. He urged statewide support for the school to be built in Charlottesville. "Mr. Baldwin, with a magnanimity only equaled by his eloquence, then came forward to invoke the House to unite in support of the University," the *Richmond Enquirer* noted in a subsequent issue. "He said, he had attempted to discharge his duty to his constituents; he had supported the pretensions of Staunton, as long as there was the slightest hope of success; but now he came forward to conjure the House to sacrifice all sectional feelings on the altar of their common country."[31]

"I am told the scene was truly affecting," Cabell wrote. "A great part of the House was in tears; and, on the rising of the House, the Eastern members hovered around Mr. Baldwin; some shook him by the hand; others solicited an introduction."[32] The next day, the bill establishing a state university passed the House of Delegates. Debate then began in the senate, where Cabell argued for its passage until an illness gripped him and he found himself unable to continue. But later in January, the senate approved the bill on a vote of 22 to 1. After months of strenuous politicking, Cabell, who saw the university as a "holy cause," had realized Jefferson's dream.[33]

The General Assembly action would put in motion the South's largest construction project to date. At the same time, one of the northern states, New York, was embarking on a massive project of its own—the building of the Erie Canal. The canal, dubbed by Jefferson "little short of madness,"[34] would nonetheless help create a unified national market economy out of the myriad hamlets and farmlands scattered across the landscape. It turned New York into a commercial colossus, just as Jefferson hoped his university would turn Charlottesville into the nation's center of intellectual inquiry. Both ultimately opened in 1825.

But first Jefferson would have to drum up support for his school. Following the General Assembly vote, he began a fight for state funding that would last years. Cabell would become Jefferson's leading ally, carrying the burden of wringing money from the state. In creating the university the legislature had authorized $15,000 annually—a woefully inadequate amount considering the $300,000 ($4.1 million today) it would actually cost to build Jefferson's grand vision. As the campus buildings, the dormitories, and the professors' pavilions went up, brick by brick, Jefferson and Cabell cajoled and pleaded with the General Assembly to keep funding flowing. The fledgling university borrowed tens of thousands of dollars. Constantly in debt, the school was dependent on the goodwill of the legislature. That meant the school's image had to be squeaky clean. Despite the amicable conclusion to the General Assembly's debate, enemies, political and religious, were always looking for reasons to shut down Jefferson's unique secular experiment. The necessity to appear as a model of decorum would color how the school reacted to student misbehavior. Professors and school officials would feel constant pressure to downplay, cover up, and gloss over student crimes and misdemeanors.

In addition to the struggle for money, Jefferson also ran into trouble in choosing one of his first professors. Dr. Thomas Cooper of Pennsylvania, whom Jefferson hailed as "the greatest man in America in the powers of his mind," was offered the chair of chemistry.[35] The job paid $1,000 a year, plus $20 for each student who attended his class. Jefferson's opponents pounced. Cooper had been jailed under the Alien and Sedition Acts during the Adams administration, making him anathema to Federalists. He was also a noted freethinker who did not believe in the immortality of the soul and believed even atheists could be good citizens. There were already concerns that Jefferson's school was barren of any religious influence, and the prospect of Cooper's appointment further stirred the wrath of Virginia's churches. The Reverend John Rice, editor of an influential Presbyterian journal, issued Jefferson a warning: "Should [the university] finally be determined to exclude Christianity, the opinion will at once be fixed that the institution is infidel." The opposition forced Cooper to resign.[36]

Jefferson, undeterred from his goal of hiring the best scholars available, dispatched the local lawyer Francis Gilmer—noted for successfully defending a "notoriously guilty" horse thief[37]—to Europe to recruit up to eight professors. Gilmer, born at the Pen Park estate in Albemarle County, was deemed educated and polished—perfect for the job.

Church leaders, especially Presbyterians, Jefferson thought, feared his university was an attempt to overthrow their "ambition and tyranny over higher education."[38] To mollify the ire of the religious establishment, Jefferson also offered to allow churches to hire their own professors, who could teach "their own tenets" on the edges of the university but independent of it. None did so. The barrage of opposition to almost every aspect of building the university—the legislature's moaning at the constant request for money and the church's loathing of Enlightenment views—caused Jefferson to despair. So pessimistic was Jefferson at the university's prospects that he wrote Cabell in 1821, "I perceive I am not to live to see it open."[39] On this point at least, Jefferson was wrong. The university opened its doors in March of 1825. But Jefferson's triumph would soon turn to travail.

"Vicious Irregularities"

On October 3, 1825, Thomas Jefferson, who had imposed his will on history so many times before, stood in a crowded room in the still unfinished Rotunda of his fledgling university to face what he described as "the most painful event" of his life.[1] With the other members of the Board of Visitors at his side, he looked upon his assembled students "with the tenderness of a father,"[2] but they responded with looks of defiance and hostility. The students stood erect. He, in contrast, was ailing and bent by age. The murmur of the youthful crowd echoed against the high ceilings. The students were tense, expecting a verbal lashing from Jefferson, not only the founder of their school but at the time the most famous man in the country. Jefferson struggled to contain his own wrath, disappointment, and frustration. The university he had toiled for decades to create was not yet seven months old and already appeared to be on the brink of failure. His students were in rebellion. His besieged professors were in revolt. The uprising would have delighted the enemies of the university, and they were many.

Jefferson, now age eighty-two, his flaming red hair now gray, stood in the freshly plastered oval room to address the student body, hoping to somehow speak the words that would rescue his school from their riotous behavior. But so wounded was the former president by their betrayal of his faith in them—he had gambled all on his belief that gentlemen did not need to be forced to do the right thing—that he could not speak. He choked on his own feeling. Margaret Bayard Smith, a visitor to Charlottesville, would later summarize student accounts of the dramatic moment this way: "His lips moved—he essayed to speak—burst into tears & sank back into his seat!—The shock was electric!"[3]

The school's first rector, the Sage of Monticello, the great architect of liberty, was crying. At the long table his fellow board members looked on at his humiliation. Near the famous author of the Declaration of Independence sat James Madison, the "Father of the Constitution." Long Jefferson's revolutionary ally and his secretary of state, Madison, like Jefferson, had retired from national politics. His face was now a permanent peanut brown from the sun that beat down on his Montpelier plantation. Madison's presidential terms had been rough—the British had burned the White House and chased his entire administration into the wilds—but America emerged from the War of 1812 with high morale, and, thanks to General Andrew Jackson, Madison had been able to squeeze Spain like an orange to obtain Florida for the young nation. Now Madison had agreed to join the school's Board of Visitors to help Jefferson run his radical experiment in education.

The other board members suffer in comparison to Jefferson and Madison, but they were prominent members of Virginia's ruling class. There was Cabell, of course, Jefferson's hardworking though hypochondriacal agent in Richmond who had arm-twisted a reluctant General Assembly into creating and funding the university. He was always ready to lend Jefferson support. And there was also General James Breckenridge, now in his sixties but willing to give his energy to the new school. Breckenridge, born near Fincastle in Virginia's western mountains, had served in the Revolution as a lad of seventeen in a rifle regiment under Nathanael Greene. After attending William and Mary College, he practiced law and had served in both the General Assembly and Congress. Another military man at the table was General John Hartwell Cocke. Born in Surry County, Virginia, in 1780, he was too late for the Revolution, but during the War of 1812 he commanded the Virginia troops that defended Richmond from British invaders. From the state's flatlands, he now lived on an estate in Fluvanna County, some thirty miles east of Monticello. The sixth board member present at the showdown with the students was the lawyer Chapman Johnson. The son of a prominent political family who had served as an aide to Breckenridge during the recent war, Johnson was now a lawyer practicing in Staunton and a member of the state senate. The final board member was the youngest, George Loyall, just thirty-six years old. Loyall represented the borough of Norfolk as a member of the House of Delegates. These are the men who witnessed Jefferson's misery. Soldiers, legislators, lawyers, and statesmen; none of them were ministers, unlike the founding board members of Yale or Harvard.

The professors in attendance, five Europeans and two American citizens, no doubt were stunned to see the great man in tears. They watched to see what Jefferson and the board would now do to rein in the defiant students. The day before, the professors had threatened to resign en masse unless "an efficient Police were immediately established in the University."[4] Two had already offered their resignations. In fact, from the very beginning Jefferson had requested that the school's "proctor" be given police powers, but the General Assembly had turned him down.

The students, who numbered sixty-three when the school opened on March 7 and whose mayhem had brought together men of such eminence to confront them, hung tightly together, shoulder to shoulder. Many of the students (whose numbers would swell to 125 during the school year) were teenagers, some as young as sixteen. Some were the sons of city merchants, and some were the sons of plantation owners or prosperous farmers; they bridled at discipline. School records show that most came from Virginia and other southern states. They came to obtain at least a gloss of education before returning to their world of rank and privilege. Just six months from home, though, their behavior had turned violent in an affront to Jefferson's lifelong belief in man's ability to control his own behavior. Their errant ways may not have surprised anyone with sons. Jefferson, however, had fathered only daughters. The recent riot, following months of unruly student behavior, including an all too common drunkenness, also threatened Jefferson's very legacy—"the child of his old age,"[5] the university he felt was critical to disseminating the education that he believed would eventually improve his country— mired for the most part in ignorance and poverty.

On September 30, 1825, three days before Jefferson ordered the students to the Rotunda, the "vicious irregularities,"[6] as he would term them, began with a bottle of piss. Student Philip Clayton of Culpeper County, Virginia, threw it through the window of Professor George Long's pavilion, one of the ten elegant brick structures Jefferson had designed to serve as campus homes for the professors. Martha Jefferson Randolph, Jefferson's daughter, in an account a week later, wrote that "a rich fool" had tossed a bottle and a "pack of cards" through Long's windows while cursing the "European professors," whom he challenged to come out "that they might be taken to the pump," an apparent threat to beat them.[7] Jefferson had recruited five of his seven professors, including Long, from Europe. He believed the best professors were to be found there and not in America, an attitude that had incensed his critics and created more enemies for the university.

As Clayton would later confess, the professors' nationality played little role in his misbehavior: he had been "excited by wine" at the time.[8] The following night, on the Lawn—the grassy expanse framed by the pavilions and rows of student rooms—a disturbance erupted. As many as fourteen students, "animated first with wine," slipped masks over their faces to hide their identity and swarmed onto the Lawn "with no intention, it is believed, but of childish noise and uproar."[9] The two American professors, John Emmet and Faculty Chairman George Tucker, dutifully stepped out into the darkness to quell the disturbance. They were outnumbered and surprised by the students' resistance. Tucker grabbed the first student he caught up to. In a twist of fate, the student, the first student apprehended in the school's first rebellion, was Wilson Miles Cary, Jefferson's own grandnephew. At the time, his identity was unknown, shielded by his mask and the darkness.

Cary, of nearby Fluvanna County, jerked himself free, only to be grabbed by Emmet. In the ensuing struggle in the dark, Emmet tore Cary's clothes. Cary punched the professor and rallied fellow students to his side with the cry "The damn'd rascal has torn my shirt."[10] Cary's fellow troublemakers, who shared his hair-trigger sense of honor, rushed to his aid—no one grabbed a gentleman by the collar. Cary himself picked up one of the bricks strewn about from the unfinished construction of the school. Others seized bricks and grabbed sticks to use as makeshift cudgels. A brick and a stick flew past Emmet's head. At some point in the fray, Professor Tucker admonished the students of "the impropriety of appearing in the character of mountebanks."[11]

William Eyre, a student from Eyreville in Northampton, Virginia, wearing a mask, also cried out, "Damn the European Professors!"[12] Emmet and Tucker each "seized an offender, demanded their names (for they could not distinguish them under their disguise), but were refused, abused, and the culprits calling on their companions for a rescue, got loose, and withdrew to their chambers," Jefferson wrote his grandson-in-law nearly two weeks later.[13] By the standards of the day, this was a riot, a full-fledged mob action intent on violence. Cary would try to justify his actions by saying he "conceived he was assaulted and therefore acted as he did"[14] in accordance with a code of honor that members of the young nation's upper class lived by, a strict code that demanded respect and treatment as a gentleman no matter the circumstance.

The day after the melee, October 2, the seven angry professors insisted that the entire student body appear before them. Their behavior had at last escalated beyond the professors' level of tolerance. Up to now, the students' unruliness had been more high jinks and hormones than high crime. Word of their spirited conduct, for example, had reached the ears of Cornelia J. Randolph, one of Jefferson's granddaughters and a lover of neighborhood gossip. "There is one shocking piece of Scandal afloat," she wrote in July 1825. "It is that Mr. Raphael's sister whom you may have remarked as a very bold impudent girl was missing one night & found at twelve o'clock in one of [the] dormitories of the students & it is said that it is not one, but many she visits, but really this is scandal of too black a dye to write."[15] In another incident, mischievous students had tugged an ox or bull to an upper story of the Rotunda, where its bellowing would serve as a testament to their ingenuity. The escapade, however, gave ammunition to Jefferson's enemies, always eager to hear of troubles at the school. "I regard it as a School of infidelity—a nursery of bad principles," huffed the Fredericksburg, Virginia, teacher George Pierson in a November 1825 letter to his brother Albert.[16] In June, some cows belonging to university employees had been "shamefully mutilated."[17] The professors asked the students to "endeavor by all means to discover the authors of such atrocity."[18] The students refused. In September, student John Marshall of Fredericksburg was accused of having a liquor party in his dorm room. Asked to identify the revelers, he "disrespectfully declined giving any evidence whatsoever."[19]

At the October 2 gathering, the professors harshly criticized the students and insisted they identify and denounce those who had rioted. Outraged at this new demand to finger their fellow scholars, the students "refused, answered the address in writing and in the rudest terms, and charged the Professors themselves with false statements," Jefferson wrote.[20] The perceived affront to their honor caused the unrest to spread among their classmates. "A Paper was handed in signed by 65 Students expressive of their determination not to act the part of Informers and of their indignation at the aspersion thrown upon them by the Faculty in expressing a belief that they were capable of such baseness," according to the faculty records. "They denied the fact of any assault having been made upon any Professor and asserted that on the contrary two Professors had attacked one student and that he was justified in making resistance. The whole language of the remonstrance was highly objectionably [sic]."[21] The insolent letter was signed by student Richard Anderson of Richmond, Virginia, and seven classmates.

According to Jefferson's own description of the blossoming revolt, "Fifty others, who were in their rooms, no ways implicated in the riot and knowing nothing about it, immediately signed the answer, making common cause with the rioters and declaring their belief of their assertions in opposition to those of the Professors."[22] In the first year of the school more than half of its inaugural class now stood firmly opposed in disobedience to the faculty. This first showdown would serve as a prelude to the next twenty years of tumult and turmoil.

Faced with growing student resistance, the professors sent a letter to the Board of Visitors, which oversaw the university, threatening their unanimous resignation unless the campus were policed. Professors Thomas Key and Long did not wait for a reply but announced their intention to resign. So upset were the professors that they were willing to break their contract and pay a penalty of $5,000. The professors, who had courageously sojourned to a small, dusty village in a country barely thirty-six years old to teach—lured by Jefferson's international reputation—were not easily scared. Now they were. Jefferson's university, newly christened, was already foundering.

Coincidentally, the Board of Visitors was scheduled to meet the next day, October 3, at the university. Jefferson had planned not to attend because of his ill health. However, the unfolding crisis threatening to undo his years of labor prompted him to take the agonizing eight-mile horseback ride over the "rough mountain-road"[23] leading from his home at Monticello to the school. Jefferson was a practical man who tolerated no nonsense or frivolity in his life—he couldn't understand the point of fiction, and even a novel as great as Sir Walter Scott's *Ivanhoe* wearied him[24]—and his students' irrational actions perplexed him. It was at this meeting that Jefferson stood and tried to express his frustration and anger at the students' behavior but was too mortified to speak.

After the tearful Jefferson sat down in despair, he turned to Chapman Johnson, saying "that he must commit to younger hands the task of saying that which he felt unable to say."[25] Henry Tutwiler, a student from Alabama who was in the room, recalled with clarity Johnson's persuasive scorn fifty-seven years later: "Those who have seen and heard this eminent lawyer will remember his dignified bearing, his bright, intelligent face, and his earnest, persuasive manner. If eloquence is to be estimated by its effects, I have never heard any that surpassed this. His glowing appeal to their honor; the withering scorn with which he denounced the outrages, were irresistible, and when asked to come forward and give in their names, without any apparent concert, there was a simultaneous rush to the table."[26] But Margaret Smith, the visitor to Charlottesville, said Johnson's speech was not the catalyst for the students' repentance. "To be sure Chapman Johnson, finding Mr J could not speak, arose & addressed them, but as one of the young men told me it was not his words, but Mr Jefferson's tears that melted their stubborn purpose."[27]

One of those who rushed forward to turn himself in was Cary, Jefferson's grandnephew. Jefferson, ill and humiliated, was now overcome with fury at the sight of his nephew. Tucker, the chairman of the faculty, recalled Jefferson's reaction: "The shock which Mr. Jefferson felt when he for the first time discovered that the efforts of the last ten years of his life had been foiled and put in jeopardy by one of his family was more than his own patience could endure, and he could not forbear from using, for the first time, the language of indignation and reproach."[28]

Armed with the names of the students—their code of silence temporarily cracked—the faculty called them in to give an account of themselves. Though no student admitted to being drunk (alcohol was forbidden in the precincts), professors suspected otherwise. Drunkenness was so common the professors had asked the Board of Visitors a few days before the riot to level a one-dollar fine against any student found intoxicated and to bar repeat offenders from the precincts. As one student would note of the school's early years, "Here nothing is more common than to see students so drunk as to be unable to walk."[29]

Arthur Smith of Suffolk, Virginia, admitted he was on the Lawn the night of the rebellion but said he took no part in the fracas and only signed the students' reply because he thought two professors had attacked a student. Philip Bolling of Buckingham County, Virginia, said he signed the paper unaware that students had thrown bricks at a professor.[30] Eyre testified that he had cried out "Damn the European Professors!" only "for fun" and "without any evil design."[31] Student Robert A. Thompson of Kanawha, Virginia, admitted he picked up a stick but said he did so because he felt Cary was under assault. In the end, the faculty recommended the Board of Visitors expel three students—Cary, Thompson, and Eyre. Eight others were admonished.

Cary, who had disgraced his famous granduncle and himself, surprised even his friends by accepting the advice of General John Cocke, who urged him to study law by working in a nearby circuit court clerk's office. Martha Jefferson Randolph, Cary's cousin, called Cary's new attitude "the most surprising conquest over his pride and love for dissipation I ever heard of."[32] (Cary would eventually become a lawyer in Fluvanna, move to Maryland, and serve in the state senate.)

The year of mayhem was a result of Jefferson's pie-in-the-sky faith in human nature. Even his old ally Francis Gilmer couldn't refrain from criticizing the former president. "The university has been very near its exit in the first few months of its birth," he wrote to John Randolph of

Roanoke. "I found all likely to perish in the beginning. . . . Scarcely a thing has been done which I should approve, and half the utility of my labours in England has been marred, by Mr. Js self-willed, and misguided mind."[33]

Jefferson wanted his students to govern themselves, and he founded the school on "the principles of avoiding too much government."[34] According to his original plan, students accused of serious wrongdoing were to appear before a student court, which would decide guilt and punishment. Meanwhile, a proctor, normally a disciplinarian, would serve as a police officer in what was then called the precincts. The university would also have its own jail so that errant gentlemen students would not have to suffer the shame and indignity of spending the night in a local jail with common miscreants and hardened criminals. But the court of students failed because its student members refused to punish their classmates. And the General Assembly, which only reluctantly funded the school's construction, declined to authorize the jail or a police officer. The efforts to create a system in which students would govern themselves were further stymied because students were under no obligation to testify against each other. As recently as March 4, 1825, the board had enacted a rule stating, "When testimony is required from a Student, it shall be voluntary, and not on oath, and the obligation to give it shall be left to his own sense of right."[35]

Now, with three students expelled, the Board of Visitors at Jefferson's urging decided to get tough. After the riotous students had given up their names and been dismissed from the Rotunda, Jefferson, with the same hand that penned the Declaration of Independence, wrote, perhaps reluctantly, a new set of rules for professors, and he admonished students on what true honor meant. Thenceforward, professors would have to take daily attendance, take notice of tardy students, and write monthly letters to parents detailing any absences. Jefferson also urged professors to "exactly and strictly" enforce existing rules.[36] But Jefferson saved the thrust of his comments for the students and what he deemed their wrongheaded notion of honor. By protecting those who had taken part in the "vicious irregularities," innocent students were only damaging their own reputations, Jefferson wrote. Telling on friends who broke the school's rules and the law was honorable, and necessary: "The Visitors are aware that a prejudice prevails too extensively among the young that it is dishonorable to bear witness one against another. . . . But this loose principal in the ethics of school-boy combinations is unworthy of mature and regulated minds, and is accordingly condemned by the laws of their country which . . . compel those who have knowledge of a fact to declare it for the purpose of justice and of the general good and safety of society."[37] Having noted that the state compels testimony for the common good, Jefferson then urged students "no longer to screen the irregular and the vicious under the respect of their cloak" and to "co-operate with the faculty in future, for preservation of order, the vindication of their own character and the reputation and usefulness of an institution which their country has so liberally established for their improvement."[38]

Jefferson and the Board of Visitors did not stop there. The university's janitor, a jack-of-all-trades position, was to become part of a more watchful administration. He was to spy on and testify against misbehaving students. Hotelkeepers, who ran the student dining halls, were coerced into becoming informants. And professors, admonished to better enforce existing rules, were to roam the precincts at night, looking to thwart bad behavior.

The board shortened the leash on students by enacting even more rules, including a requirement that letters be written to parents when students were habitually absent from the dorms at night, a prohibition on hotelkeepers against providing entertainment to students, a stipulation of punishment for students who allowed misbehavior in their rooms even if they didn't take part, the bestowal of police powers on the faculty, the banning of masks or disguises, and a requirement that students stop and give their name to any professor who asked.

Jefferson's daughter Martha applauded the imposition of these "pretty rigid" rules on the university and even hoped the riot would do the school some good: "I think so far from regretting it that it has eventually placed the institution upon a much more solid foundation by giving discipline which it certainly wanted, and expelling some who have kept it constantly in confusion. [E]verything is going on quietly and smoothly and likely to continue so. [S]ome few remain who ought to have been expelled, but for want of legal evidence they could not be laid hold of, but they are known and will be closely watched."[39]

The university's first riot had been dealt with. New "severer laws" were in place. Students and professors alike had been lectured. But Jefferson had seen his precious experiment in education nearly die in its infancy. The university depended on General Assembly funding, which itself depended on the public's sense that the university was being run decorously and was serving poor and rich alike. Casual student violence by hell-raisers, a riot, and a faculty threat to resign had all undermined the institution and played into the hands of its critics.

The fate of Jefferson's university held implications far beyond the hardscrabble hamlet of Charlottesville. In Boston, George Ticknor, a professor of Spanish literature and language at Harvard who had befriended Jefferson the previous decade, was watching the former president's experiment with keen interest. Like Jefferson, Ticknor wanted American schools to shed the hidebound British-style curriculum and give students choices, just as universities in Europe were doing. "I am much pleased to see by the Newspapers, that your University is going into Operation," Ticknor had written to Madison on March 29, 1825, three weeks after the school opened: "It is a great & very important experiment; & the Colleges of New England, are, I think, deeply interested in its success. Our system of instruction, which differs very little from the system that existed here a century ago, is but very imperfectly suited to our present condition. We must change before long, but the great difficulty is, to know, how we shall change, & what we shall do. . . . I look upon your great experiment in Virginia as very valuable."[40] However, with Ticknor's fellow professors thwarting his reform efforts, he managed only to win permission to reform the curriculum of his own department. He therefore looked to Virginia for inspiration and support to achieve his goal of more far-reaching reforms. "I do not know, whether I should have succeeded in producing any movement, if you had not begun your University of Virginia on principles so truly liberal and wise," Ticknor wrote Madison in November 1825. "On all accounts, therefore, I wish you the most entire success. Indeed, as in such cases the whole must rise or fall together, in the flourishing condition of your University, will be the cause of the same condition in ours."[41] In short, Ticknor was saying the success of curricular reform at Harvard depended on the success of Jefferson's university. Among other innovations Harvard would watch closely was Jefferson's insistence from the very beginning on written examinations. Most colleges of the day required students to take oral exams. Yale turned to written exams in 1830, as did Harvard in 1857.

Jefferson thought his new emphasis on discipline had saved his university and disarmed his enemies. He was wrong: the school's future was far from certain. The enemies of the ex-president and his university were legion. Many still hated him for his politics. Many among the clergy considered him an infidel, and their suspicions about his godlessness seemed to be confirmed by his creation of a university that had no chapel, was affiliated with no church, and had no professor of divinity, unlike all other American colleges. Others opposed the university because Jefferson had placed Europeans in the professorships, a perceived insult to American scholarship. Still others were upset that Jefferson had maneuvered the location of the school to Charlottesville instead of nearby Staunton or Lexington, or even Richmond.

Tales of Horror

Edgar Allan Poe was one of the youngest students to arrive on the university precincts in 1826. Like most students he traveled over a series of rough roads and ragged paths; it took twelve hours to ride the sixty miles from Richmond to Charlottesville by horseback. Rough-hewn tree trunks served as footbridges over streams and rivers. The town of Charlottesville, located in the center of the rolling hills and mountains of Albemarle County (with a population of about 9,000 whites and 11,500 black slaves), was a collection of small homes, busy hotels, taverns, a courthouse, and a stone jail. This was the bustling and noisy epicenter of an otherwise sleepy frontier: blacksmiths hammered and wagons trundled through town while gristmills ground corn and wheat. Crowds gathered at the courthouse to watch courtroom dramas unfold. The scream of sawmills split the air, which was filled with smoke and the pungent smell of distilleries and tanneries.

Though he would become an offbeat American icon, celebrated and unique, at Jefferson's school Poe rapidly became just one of the crowd—drinking and gambling and skirting the rules. Not one to bloody his own knuckles, he witnessed many brawls, sometimes gruesome. The horrific, bare-knuckle battles he saw up close were nearly as brutal as the fiction he would one day pen. He filled letters home with sharp observations of university life, including accounts of his classmates in combat.

"We have had a great many fights up here lately—The faculty expelled Wickliffe last night for general bad conduct," the seventeen-year-old wrote his foster father on September 21, 1826. He continued,

But more especially for biting one of the student's arms with whom he was fighting—I saw the whole affair—it took place before my door—Wickliffe was much the stronger but not content with that—after getting the other completely in his power, he began to bite—I saw the arm afterwards—and it was really a serious matter. It was bitten from the shoulder to the elbow—and it is likely that pieces of flesh as large as my hand will be obliged to be cut out. He is from Kentucky—the same one that was in suspension when you were up here some time ago—Give my love to Ma and Miss Nancy.[1]

Tradition holds that Poe's room was number 13, located on what was called the Western Range. Jefferson had laid out his campus in four orderly rows of dorms that ran on a north to south axis. One row of twenty-eight student rooms faced the grassy expanse called the Lawn from the west, and a nearly identical row of twenty-six faced the Lawn from the east. A covered walkway ran along the front of the Lawn rooms, supported by rows of stately pillars. Parallel to the row of Lawn rooms were the Range rooms, which faced outward, away from the Lawn. Poe's room faced a field where today the school's main libraries are located. Interspersed among the Lawn rooms were ten pavilions where the professors lived. Interspersed among the Range rooms were the six "hotels" where students ate their meals. At the north end of the Lawn stood the grand Rotunda, modeled on Rome's Pantheon. The Rotunda provided space for the library and lecture halls. Though located at the north end of the precincts, the Rotunda served as the heart and spiritual center of the university. Jefferson had obsessed over the appearance of his university, but despite his intimate familiarity with its layout, he once opened a pavilion door to leave, only to find himself stepping into a closet.[2]

Overall, the precise, compact design at the heart of the forty-four-acre campus was a manifestation of Jefferson's intent to create an intimate community where young scholars could live shoulder to shoulder with their professors, insulated from the brutishness of the yeoman's life. (As usual, though, Jefferson's critics found cause to complain: "One of the most popular objections to the Institution, I find is the expence added by what is called the ornamental style of the Architecture," Madison noted in 1823.)[3]

But there was no escaping the grittiness of the early nineteenth century. The Lawn was a rugged, two-hundred-foot-wide, stony slope of ragged grass and dirt where cows, pigs, sheep, chickens, and wild dogs roamed and defecated. The privies, located between the Range and Lawn rooms, stank, especially in the heat of the Charlottesville summers. Crowds of slave children hung about the complex. Dust rose from the nearby road that ran between the school and Charlottesville. The university had more than two hundred hearths: black chimney smoke from the hotels and dorm fireplaces blew across the university, while flies swarmed about the piles of garbage tossed out from the hotel kitchens. The pungent odor of the school's stables was inescapable. Students and professors alike bathed infrequently, sharing a bathhouse located outside the immediate area of the Lawn. A whipping post for slaves stood ready at the edge of the precincts.

This was the university, raw and unfinished, where Poe arrived on a cold day in February 1826, young, ambitious, and eager to start a new life after a Dickensian childhood. His parents, an alcoholic father and a high-strung young mother, had been traveling actors who often left Poe and his brother with friends. His father drank excessively and eventually abandoned the family. His mother died young of tuberculosis. Poe, only two, was taken in by the Allans, a well-to-do Richmond family. John Allan, a merchant, was an uneducated man who had done well for himself. He was a social climber who understood that an education was a boost up the economic ladder. He saw in Poe a chance to bring a family member into the ranks of scholarship.

Poe came to the university already polished by a brief education in England. He had read widely for his age and had studied French and Latin. In Richmond, he studied more Latin, as well as Greek, and used a tutor to prepare for the university. In Charlottesville, he enrolled in the School of Ancient Languages and the School of Modern Languages. While most students enrolled in three schools, Poe's foster father, a self-made man, was tight with his money and wanted Poe to learn self-reliance; Poe could only afford to attend two schools. (Students had to pay fifty dollars to attend the lectures of one professor, sixty dollars for two professors, and seventy-five dollars for three.)

While many of his classmates fought, gambled, and drank, indifferent and inattentive to their course work, Poe excelled. He joined the Jefferson Literary and Debating Society, where he once argued on the topic "Heat and Cold." He also sketched highly ornate figures in charcoal on the walls of his dorm room. Once, a classmate with whom Poe had chipped in to buy a copy of Byron's *Poems* walked in to find Poe drawing Byron's image on his ceiling in crayon. The life-size figure was a replica of the book's engraved frontispiece of Byron. Byron's image, peering down through the soft candlelight, would have inspired the brooding young man as he lay in bed and fantasized about winning glory as a writer.[4] Poe also hiked the wooded hills around Charlottesville and possibly supped with Jefferson at Monticello, where the school's founder habitually invited students to dine on Sundays. In Professor George Blaettermann's modern languages courses, Poe could solve difficult translation problems that defeated his peers. Blaettermann took note of the young scholar and occasionally invited him to his pavilion. Poe, Blaettermann said, often showed up, "especially when we had young ladies visiting us."[5] At least one classmate found him to be a loner: "He wore a melancholy face always and even his smile,—for I do not remember ever to have seen him laugh,—seemed to be forced."[6]

But Poe's college life was not a smooth one: he was locked in a battle of wills with his autocratic foster father. Poe demanded more money, but Allan refused. Surrounded by rich young men, Poe turned to gambling—a dismissible offense—possibly as a way to pick their pockets. He also learned to drink hard. "I led a very dissipated life—the college at that period being shamefully dissolute," Poe later wrote. "Took the first honors, however, and came home greatly in debt."[7] A promissory note signed by Poe on December 14, 1826, shows he owed the Dan S. Mosby Company $41.36. Other reports suggest he owed an astounding gambling debt of $2,000.

As Poe furtively gambled and lost in the dorm rooms—probably at card games such as whist and loo—the routine violence continued. "There have been several fights since you were here," Poe wrote Allan in May 1826. "One between Turner Dixon and [Robert] Blow from Norfolk excited more interest than any I have seen, for a common fight is so trifling an occurrence that no notice is taken of it—Blow got much the advantage in the scuffle—but Dixon posted him in very indecent terms." To "post" someone was to accuse an opponent of dishonorable behavior in writing and then to post the note in public. Whatever Dixon wrote in his post outraged Blow's hometown supporters. "The whole Norfolk party rose in arms," Poe wrote, "—& nothing was talked off [*sic*] for a week, but Dixon's charge & Blow's explanation—every pillar in the University was white with scratched paper." Poe went on to describe the escalating fight: "Dixon made a physical attack upon Arthur Smith one of Blow's Norfolk friends—and a 'very fine fellow.' [H]e struck him with a large stone on one side of his head—whereupon Smith drew a pistol (which are all the fashion here) and had it not miss-fire [*sic*]— would have put an end to the controversy."[8]

The incident that Poe chronicled was routine. Violence and drunk-enness, for many reasons, were endemic. During the year, student Ster-ling F. Edmunds of Brunswick County, Virginia, whipped student Charles Peyton of Albemarle County, Virginia, with a cowhide. Ed-munds had lost $200 playing all fours, a popular card game, in Peyton's dorm room. Edmunds accused Peyton of cheating. Later hearing that an affronted Peyton planned to cane him, Edmunds struck first with his whip. In November, two other Virginia students, Turner Dixon (of Dixon vs. Blow notoriety) and Livingston Lindsay, were expelled for trying to fight a duel, a criminal act and the most odious offense a student could commit in the university's eyes. Two drunken students, William Cross of Albemarle County and William Emmet of New York were rep-rimanded for trying to waylay a professor's carriage as he returned to his pavilion from church. The violence became so widespread that a grand jury was convened at the university's request to end the "disturbances." As Poe recounted in a letter to his foster father, "The Grand Jury met and put the students in a terrible fright—so much so that the lectures were unattended—and those whose names were up on the Sheriff's list—traveled off into the woods & mountains—taking their beds and provisions along with them—there were about 50 on the list—so you may suppose the College was very well thinned."[9] The student body, in this second year of the university's existence, numbered 177, and now

50 of them were fugitives from the law. The beleaguered faculty debated "urging the necessity of a competent police for this university."[10] As William Wertenbaker, the school's librarian, noted, the university had descended into a state of "insubordination, lawlessness, and riot."[11]

In the middle of a year of turmoil and tumult, calamity struck. Jefferson fell gravely ill, just when the university needed his reasoned guidance the most. He was eighty-three years old, far beyond the life expectancy of the time, and his six-foot-two-inch frame was now "bent and emaciated." The university's professor of medicine, Robley Dunglison, had become Jefferson's personal physician shortly after arriving the year before, and he had treated the ex-president's enlarged prostate, which caused Jefferson to urinate frequently. Now, the problem became more serious: Jefferson ate less and suffered from diarrhea. No longer could he ride his favorite horse, Eagle, along the rugged road that led from Monticello to the university. On June 24, Jefferson wrote Dunglison a note begging the doctor to come see him. Jefferson, his strength waning, lacked the power to rise from his bed.

Jefferson's mind, even as he lay dying, was consumed by the potential failure of his university. For a decade, work on the school had enlivened the old man; he had obsessed over the minutest details of its construction, even spying on the hundreds of workmen through a telescope placed atop Monticello. Overseer Edmund Bacon recalled the day that Jefferson himself laid out the very foundations of the school:

> An Irishman named Dinsmore and I went along with him. As we passed through Charlottesville, I went to old Davy Isaacs' store and got a ball of twine, and Dinsmore found some shingles and made some pegs and we all went on to the old field together. Mr. Jefferson looked over the ground some time and then stuck down a peg. He struck the very first peg in that building, and then directed me where to carry the line, and I stuck the second. He carried one end of the line, and I the other, in laying off the foundation of the University. He had a little rule in his pocket that he always carried with him, and with this he measured off the ground and laid off the entire foundation and then set the men at work.[12]

Professor Tucker marveled at Jefferson's stamina as the buildings rose and the professors and students arrived:

> In getting the university into operation, he seemed to have regained the activity and assiduity of his youth. Every thing was looked into, every thing was ordered by him. He suggested the remedy for every difficulty and made the selection in every choice of expediency. Two or three times a week he rode down to the establishment to give orders to the proctor, and to watch the progress of the work still unfinished. Nor were his old habits of hospitality forgotten. His invitations to the professors and their families were frequent, and every Sunday some four or five of the students dined with him.[13]

Student Henry Tutwiler had similar recollections of Jefferson as a hardworking octogenarian:

> We use to see him afterwards as he passed our room on the eastern Range in his almost daily visits to the University. He was now in his 80-third year, and this ride of eight or ten miles on horseback over a rough mountain-road shows the deep interest with which he watched over this 'child of his old age,' and why he preferred the more endearing title of Father to that of Founder. This is also shown in the frequent intercourse which he kept up with the Faculty and students.[14]

The dying Jefferson now lay on his narrow, canopied bed in the bedroom where he had often sought sanctuary. His bouts of diarrhea had lessened, though he probably suffered from severe dehydration and, according to Dunglison, his "powers were failing."[15]

"Until the 2nd and 3rd of July he spoke freely of his approaching death; made all his arrangements with his grandson, Mr. Randolph, in regard to his private affairs, and expressed his anxiety for the prosperity of the University," Dunglison wrote. Jefferson fell into a stupor on July 2, though he would occasionally regain consciousness. By July 3, his moments awake were few. At seven that evening, Jefferson woke, saw Dunglison, and said: "Ah! Doctor are you still there?" Jefferson's voice was hoarse and almost inaudible. "Is it the 4th?" Whether or not Jefferson could hear him, Dunglison replied: "It soon will be."[16]

Jefferson's grandson-in-law Nicholas Trist sat at Jefferson's side at eleven that night and again Jefferson asked: "This is the Fourth?" Trist, knowing Jefferson's desire to die on the Fourth of July—the fiftieth anniversary of the nation's birth—ignored the question because he couldn't bear to tell Jefferson that the Fourth was still an hour away.

But Jefferson immediately inquired again, "This is the Fourth?" Trist, torn by his grandfather-in-law's suffering, nodded.

"Ah," Jefferson sighed, "just as I wished." Jefferson's strength carried him to the next day. He died at 12:50 p.m. on July 4, 1826. His university was a mere sixteen months old, still an infant. In nearby Charlottesville, cannons boomed. At the courthouse, the bell tolled to signal "that the spirit of the author of the Declaration of Independence had taken its flight from its tenement of clay."[17]

Jefferson had directed that his funeral be simple, "without any pomp or ceremony whatever."[18] On July 5, a warm, rainy day, his coffin was carried from Monticello down the mountain to the small family cemetery at its base. About forty mourners arrived to see the coffin resting on narrow planks across the open grave. Among the small group were his university professors, wearing crape on their left arms, and a small contingent of students. Andrew K. Smith, a mourner, recalled seeing Poe, whom he described as "a high minded and honorable young man, though easily persuaded to his wrong."[19] In his eulogy, friend and lawyer William Wirt claimed that Jefferson clasped his hands and said as he died: "Nunc dimittis," or "Now lettest thou thy servant depart," quoting Luke 2:29.[20] Details of the burial were not made public, but some fifteen hundred people made their way up the mountain to find, to their disappointment, the grave already filled.

Jefferson penned his own epitaph, leaving instructions that his obelisk was to contain "the following inscription and not a word more":

Here was buried Thomas Jefferson, Author of the Declaration of American Independence, Of the Statute of Virginia for Religious Freedom and Father of the University of Virginia.[21]

The students at his university mourned him, recalling him as a humble man whose charm and empathy put even the most awkward young student at ease. "I well remember the first time I saw Mr. Jefferson," Tutwiler reminisced. "It was in 1825, in the Proctor's office, wither I had gone with some students on business. A tall, venerable gentleman, in plain but neat attire, entered the room and, bowing to the students, took his seat quietly in one corner. . . . I was struck by his plain appearance, and simple, unassuming manners."[22] But despite their admiration of Jefferson and their grief over his death, within several weeks, the students resumed the behavior that would threaten the existence of his university. The drinking and gambling began again, as did a widespread disregard for authority. The students were unconcerned about the consequence of their behavior; many no doubt knew they were destined to lead by birthright. Student Jerman Baker of Richmond was caught trying to explode a bomb made of a quart bottle full of gunpowder outside a dorm room. A mob of students attacked the house of a Mr. Crawford and ripped the clothes off one of his slave girls. Student George Hoffman of New York explained that students assaulted the girl because they assumed "that she was one of the women who had infected the students with disease." Crawford agreed to pay the students ten dollars as a "compromise," an act that suggested she was a prostitute in his employ.[23] Students broke out their forbidden decks of cards and played games of chance, such as all fours, at two dollars a hand. Poe was one of the suspected gamblers, and professors called him in for questioning.

Scholars amid Scofflaws

Professors, who had anticipated that most of their work would take place within the confines of a classroom, were now forced to capture miscreants, judge their guilt, and mete out punishment. With students refusing to form a court to punish each other, the task of school discipline fell to the professors and, more particularly, to Faculty Chairman George Tucker. The task required steely determination—or, as Cabell once grumbled, steel of another sort: "I am particularly anxious to be informed on the best mode of governing a large mass of students without the use of the bayonet."[1]

The professors numbered eight in 1826, the school's second year. They were a motley collection of eccentric and brilliant personalities. To understand them is to understand how the school and students were shaped in these crucial years. These were the men Jefferson had chosen to guide the school to preeminence.

One of the two Americans on the faculty at the university's inception was John Patton Emmet, not yet twenty-nine years old when the school opened its doors to students. He was best known to students for the menagerie of wild animals he kept in his pavilion. Born in Ireland on April 8, 1796, Emmet was the son of Thomas Emmet, a ringleader in the Irish rebellion of 1798 who was sent to prison in Scotland. After his father's release, John Emmet moved with his family to New York in 1804. Emmet attended the U.S. Military Academy at West Point, where he also became assistant professor of mathematics until his health weakened in 1817.

After spending a year in Naples, Italy, recovering, Emmet returned to America and in 1822 earned a medical degree from the New York College of Physicians and Surgeons. He practiced in Charleston, South Carolina, where he delivered a series of lectures on chemistry that became so popular he caught the attention of the University of Virginia founders. He arrived in Charlottesville to assume the post of chemistry professor as a perfect bachelor and populated his house with snakes, a white owl, and a tame bear that freely roamed the house and garden. But after he married Professor George Tucker's niece, Mary Byrd Tucker of Bermuda, the snakes were banished, the owl set free, and the bear put on a dinner plate. A grand experimenter, Emmet ran tests on everything from raising silkworms to curing hams. Cornelia Randolph, Jefferson's granddaughter, seemed fascinated with him when she wrote, in her folksy, precise manner, to her sister Ellen Randolph Coolidge: "Dr. Emmet is an irishman complete, warm in his likings & dislikes; fiery, & so impetuous even in lecturing that his students complain his words are too rapid for their apprehension; they cannot follow him quick enough; to which he answers, they must catch his instruction as it goes, he cannot wait for any man's understanding, in conversation his words tumble out heels over head so that he is continually making bulls & blunders and to crown all has much of the brogue when he becomes animated."[2]

Tucker, the other American and known to his colleagues as a most wretched novelist, was a native of Bermuda and a member of the U.S. Congress when Jefferson tapped him to be his professor of moral philosophy. He was the first to feel the burden of the former president's lax attitude toward discipline. With his other innovations in higher education, Jefferson had made no room for a president at his university, instead setting up a system in which members of the faculty would each year elect from among themselves a chairman who would serve as chief administrator of all school business outside the classroom. Jefferson thought a president would be a barrier to intimacy among students and professors. And, of course, presidents of other universities were typically religious leaders, and Jefferson saw no advantage in putting a churchman in charge of his secular school. The chairman was to serve a term of one year before passing the title on to the next professor. On April 12,

1825, the professors held their first faculty meeting and, in Tucker's absence, elected him chairman. They felt that, as an American, he might have a better understanding of the students. Also, Tucker was fifty years old, by far the eldest professor.

Tucker had served under Bermuda's chief barrister before moving to Williamsburg, Virginia, to study law at the College of William and Mary. Though a lawyer and a politician by trade—he served as a state legislator before moving on to Congress—Tucker also harbored lifelong literary ambitions, which became the impetus for weighty socioeconomic tomes and mediocre novels. One of his nonfiction works was titled *Theory of Money and Banks*, and when students saw him riding by on his horse, they occasionally proclaimed, "Yonder goes dear old Tucker on Money and Banks."[3] As for Tucker's fiction, Dunglison was so appalled by it that when he began editing the university's first magazine, the *Museum*, and Tucker offered to write short stories for it, Dunglison wrote a note of complaint to Cabell, the Board of Visitors member.

Like most of the professors, Tucker endured a rocky relationship with the students. Once, students besieged his pavilion (on the southern end of the Western Lawn) and smashed bottles against the front wall after listening at the door of a faculty meeting and hearing Tucker argue for maximum punishment for some young offenders. "Mr. Tucker is not much liked they say," gossipy Cornelia Randolph wrote in August 1825. "His eccentricity of character does not please and in his capacity of professor he is still less thought of, at least by students." Tucker's personality—he was quick with a joke, fond of racy conversation, and employed a veritable arsenal of anecdotes—also grated on Blaettermann, professor of modern languages. "Professor Blaettermann, what is the meaning of rigmarole?" Tucker asked him once. "I don't know whether I can give you the exact meaning of the word," Blaettermann replied humorlessly, "but if one will go to hear one or two of your lectures, he will have a good idea of its meaning."[4]

George Long was one of the European professors the public was aghast to find Jefferson had hired. Jefferson had sent his friend Francis Gilmer to England to recruit professors, and when news reached the United States that Jefferson's new university had solicited Europeans, newspaper critics railed. "Mr. Jefferson might as well have said that his *taverns* and *dormitories* should not be built with American bricks and have sent to Europe for them as to import a group of Professors," blustered the *Boston Courier.* "Mr. Gilmer could have fully discharged his mission, with half the trouble and expense, by a short trip to New England." The *Philadelphia Gazette* appended: "Or, we may be permitted to add, by a still shorter trip to Philadelphia. . . . This sending of a Commission to Europe, to engage professors for a new University, is we think one of the greatest insults the American people have received."[5]

Long was the first lecturer to arrive at the university. After sailing from England to New York, the professor of ancient languages took stagecoaches south and into Virginia, along the way meeting what would prove to be a lifelong love: American cornbread. When he showed up at the university, still under construction, in December 1824, he found it "was without inhabitants and looked like a deserted city."[6]

Long, whom the students called Colonel and apparently liked despite a certain sarcastic tone in the classroom, initially took his meals at one of the university hotels, the one run by a Mrs. Gray. There, the handsome but short professor wooed Harriet Selden, the widow of an Arkansas judge killed in a duel not long before. The courtship prompted students to compose a poem, which they recited within hearing of the amorous couple: "Harriet wants but little here below / But wants that little Long."[7]

A mere twenty-four years old when classes began, Long astonished Jefferson with his youth when he visited Monticello for the first time, according to a scrap of dialogue left to posterity.

"Are you the new professor of ancient languages?" Jefferson asked as he came out to greet his guest.

"I am, sir," Long answered.

"You are very young."

"I shall grow older, sir."

Jefferson smiled, and after an evening of conversation with Long, the former president was writing letters praising him to his acquaintances.[8]

The second European to arrive was Blaettermann, a cranky, brusque German in his early forties who had joined Napoleon Bonaparte's army before it marched on Moscow. Blaettermann claimed he only survived starvation in the pell-mell flight from Russia by strapping chocolate cakes to his body with strips of cloth. Born in 1782 in Langensalza, Germany, Blaettermann was destined to be a brilliant linguist, though not a very pleasant one. He studied at sundry European schools, including Leipzig and Heidelberg; taught Latin, French, German, and Italian; and spoke Spanish as well. After moving to London, he met and married Elizabeth Charlotte Dean, herself a gifted linguist who had served as governess to the children of the British governor of Gibraltar—an impressive background that would not prevent Blaettermann from publicly horsewhipping her later at Jefferson's university.

Alone among the university's first professors, Blaettermann had asked for the job before being solicited. He wrote Jefferson a letter (in French) in 1819, shortly after hearing about Jefferson's plans for the school, pitching himself as the ideal candidate for the modern languages professorship. Jefferson checked with his friend George Ticknor, the Harvard professor who was very soon to bring Jefferson's educational innovations to Cambridge, and after Ticknor replied that he had heard Blaettermann highly praised, Jefferson hired him.

Once at the university, Blaettermann proved a poor teacher, arousing the ire of his students, who at various times assaulted him, pelted him with lead shot, besieged his house, and petitioned to have him dismissed. Enrollment in the modern languages classes plummeted—though in fairness to Blaettermann, he was trying to teach an entire Spanish class with only three textbooks to share—and many students hired tutors to teach them languages. Cornelia Randolph, usually an astute observer, offered her scarcely believable impression that Blaettermann was popular with his students, but her views may have been colored by the fact that the professor was giving her famous grandfather private lessons in the Anglo-Saxon tongue. But Cornelia pulled no punches when it came to Blaettermann's wife: "As we become better acquainted with all of the professors & their wives we like them better with the exception of Mrs. Blatterman [*sic*] who from all accounts is a vulgar virago; indeed, she is one to whom you may apply the whole of Richard's description of his mistress's maid without speaking more harshly than she deserves

'There's not such a b——in King George's dominion
She's peevish, she's thievish, she's ugly, she's old
And a liar, and a fool & a slut & a scold.'"

Cornelia concluded her attack by noting, "Not one word is there here too much, for if she does not steal it is probably because she has no occasion to do so." Cornelia elsewhere noted of the couple, "The Blattermans [*sic*] are too low to relish any but vulgar society & are scarcely on speaking terms with the professors & their wives & daughters."[9]

The remaining three European professors, Long's fellow Englishmen, arrived in America together. Natural philosophy professor Charles Bonnycastle, mathematics professor Thomas Key, and professor of medicine Robley Dunglison had sailed on an "old log" of a ship named the *Competitor* and promptly found themselves swept up in one of the most violent storms to roil the Atlantic waters off the southern English coast in decades. After a months-long trip, they arrived at Charlottesville in March 1825, much to Jefferson's relief, but too late to begin classes in February as he had intended.

Bonnycastle, twenty-nine years old, was the son of the renowned mathematician John Bonnycastle and was educated at the Royal Military Academy of Woolwich. Almost morbidly shy, he was known on at least one occasion to have leapt a fence in Charlottesville and walked through the mud to avoid having to talk to passing students. The ever-observant Cornelia Randolph concluded that "he is a nervous man & queer tempered and does not as other people do."[10] Another woman, a Mrs. Beirne, who lived within the precincts in the school's early days, simply described Bonnycastle as "amiable, gentlemanlike and charming in his manners."[11]

A bachelor when he arrived in Charlottesville, Bonnycastle put aside his shyness and began courting the ladies almost immediately, and with success: he married a young American woman and had several children. One of his students wrote that Bonnycastle was often so deep in thought that he would not notice when his children would play and cavort around him.

Thomas Key, twenty-six years old when he arrived, had earned a master of arts degree at Trinity College, Cambridge, where he came to know Long. Little is known of Key's tenure at the University of Virginia—beyond the fact that he once kicked Blaettermann during a contentious faculty meeting—because he became the first professor to quit. He cited the local climate's unsuitability to his health as the reason for leaving, though others suspected that the constant student unrest hastened his departure. Cornelia Randolph described him as "much beloved" and a "good hearted man," "tho odd tempered."[12] After Key's resignation, however, Cornelia's brother-in-law, Joseph Coolidge, wrote of him that "he is one of those Englishmen who have succeeded in making their nation hated in every part of the known world!"[13]

The third English professor to sail to America aboard the *Competitor*, the twenty-six-year-old Dunglison, never suffered from Cornelia's acid pen. "We are more & more pleased with Dr. Dunglison both as a man & a physician," she wrote, adding moreover that he was "certainly" a great doctor.[14] Dunglison was born in Keswick, England, on January 4, 1798, and received his medical degree in London in 1819. A "benevolent, public-spirited character," he was known for his charitable works and in later years for promoting raised-letter books for the blind.[15]

He became great friends with Jefferson and Madison, characterizing Jefferson as the more imaginative of the two and Madison as exercising better judgment. Dunglison frequently dined with Madison. "In my latest visits to him," he recalled, "when confined to the bed or sofa in the next room, he would invite me to take his place at table; and call out, that if I did not pass the wine more freely, he would 'cashier' me!"[16] He was a prodigious writer, and some of his works became widely popular. His major triumph was his book titled *Human Physiology*, which became pivotal in the history of American medical science. Conceived as a textbook for his students at the University of Virginia, it was dedicated to Madison.

Finally, John Tayloe Lomax would become the eighth professor, arriving in time for the school's second year. He was hired as the uni-

versity's first professor of law. Born in Port Tobago, Virginia, he studied at St. John's College in Annapolis, Maryland, graduating at the age
of sixteen. He was practicing law in Fredericksburg, Virginia, when
he was recruited by Jefferson to take one of the school's most sensitive posts—the chair of the law department. Jefferson felt that only an
American could teach American law. Lomax's skills at cross-examining
miscreant students would later serve him well when he became a Virginia circuit judge. Unlike the other professors, Lomax appears to have
had pleasant relations with students.[17]

While these professors formed the front line in teaching and disci-
plining students, the members of the Board of Visitors were the bosses.
And they were also well-known leaders in Virginia: Madison, Cabell,
Johnson, Breckenridge, and Cocke. To their ranks the governor had
added former president James Monroe. Just as Madison had been President Jefferson's secretary of state, Monroe had served Madison in the
same capacity. And like his fellow Virginians, he had revolutionary credentials: he had crossed the Delaware River with Washington and been
wounded by the Hessians at the battle of Trenton. During the War of
1812, it was Monroe who served as President Madison's scout, riding
out to determine how close the approaching British were to the capital.
And just three years before joining the Board of Visitors, Monroe had
enunciated what is now known as the Monroe Doctrine. In retirement,
he had pledged to help Madison strengthen Jefferson's university.

Following two years of violence, the Visitors were sick of student
unrest and eager to suppress lawbreakers. They showed no restraint in
imposing a plethora of new, harsher, and sometimes petty rules. The
Visitors met in October 1826—less than three months after Jefferson's
death—and began a weeklong orgy of rule writing. First they elected
Madison to replace Jefferson as the new rector. Then they started their
rule making with the library. Previously, students had stolen some library books and damaged others; now they would have to pay ten cents
a day for late books and pay for any damage to the library or its books
and suffer punishment. Previously, students had given sanctuary to and
supported their expelled classmates. Now the board required students
to ostracize suspended and dismissed classmates. Previously, students

had boarded in questionable neighborhoods free from professors' surveillance. Now students who boarded outside the precincts would be required to tell the proctor where they lived. Students could no longer choose dorm rooms or at which "hotel" they would eat. Hotelkeepers were now prohibited from serving students "luxurious" food. In its toughest action, the Visitors voted to ask the legislature to establish a bona fide court at the university with the power to compel testimony and arrest and punish students. The Visitors also asked for power to jail students who broke university regulations. They wanted school rules to be treated as state law.

The Visitors hoped these new rules would mollify the professors. As noted in the minutes of their meeting, "The Visitors are the more encouraged in this hope, from the circumstance that they are now endeavoring to introduce some radical changes into the government of the University, which may secure more order than has heretofore prevailed, & may relieve the professors from some of their more irksome duties. The ensuing winter will probably ascertain how far their efforts at reform will be crowned with success."[18]

As the first tumultuous year was ending, Jefferson had implored students to show real honor and end their misbehavior. He had asked that the rules in place be enforced and had enacted new but relatively mild rules. Now, as a second rowdy year was coming to a close, the Visitors were going a step further, clamping down, issuing tougher rules, and threatening imprisonment. Clearly the university was not working. The troublesome students, self-absorbed and remarkably cruel, appeared impossible to control. The Visitors were gambling that the new rules would act as a needed yoke. The students would learn, and Jefferson's university would succeed. "The Youth of the Country cannot learn too early to respect the laws," the Visitors concluded.[19]

Poe, whose gambling was never discovered by professors, left the university in December 1826, dead broke but better educated. He would never return. His classmates had proven to be better gamblers. Like most students of the day, he spent only one year at the school. He never received a certificate because he skipped final exams. He enrolled in and subsequently left the U.S. Military Academy at West Point, which

Jefferson had established as president in 1802. While Poe would go on to fame as a writer of tales of horror, the university in Charlottesville would continue to gain notoriety for its wickedness. The Visitors forged even more fanatical rules. The students responded with rot, riot, and rebellion. Jefferson's dream of a community of self-governing scholars was over.

"A Most Villainous Compound"

In the course of a duel, pistols were often shot in the air or combatants aimed merely to wound each other to satisfy their offended honor. Unlike most duels, though, the one about to unfold on this mild spring day promised to end in death. The showdown between students Louis Wigfall of South Carolina and Charles Hamer of Mississippi was to be a "duel of an unusually savage kind."[1] The students planned to shoot at each other with rifles mounted on rests from a distance of a mere ten paces. At such close range, and with the accuracy of steadied rifles, the outcome would almost certainly be fatal for one and possibly both.

At the heart of the argument between the two young men was a woman, the alluring Miss Ann Leiper. (Most upper-class women of the time, including Miss Leiper, were put on pedestals by southern men; though women had access to higher education and were encouraged to be literate, proponents of educating women often stressed "its usefulness as preparation for marriage, motherhood, and domestic life."[2] Even Jefferson, despite his farseeing views, believed women should be taught how to keep house and raise children. Dancing, drawing, and music were also acceptable subjects for women. There was no room for women at Jefferson's university.) Professor Bonnycastle had hosted a party attended by Wigfall, Hamer, and Miss Leiper. Miss Leiper had promised Wigfall a dance. Flirtatiously, to Hamer she promised the honor of escorting her home. But as Leiper prepared to leave the party, Wigfall approached and reminded her of the promised dance. When she refused, he "very gallantly seized her hand and pulled her towards the room."[3]

In front of the other partygoers, including the women, Hamer scolded Wigfall for his rudeness. Wigfall silently seethed. Hamer had berated him in public, an affront to Wigfall's honor as heinous as a slap in the face, made all the worse by the presence of women.

The next day, Wigfall demanded that Hamer "retract" the insult. Hamer refused, saying he would only take back his statement if Miss Leiper herself agreed that Wigfall had not acted rudely. Not surprisingly, Wigfall challenged Hamer to a duel, and Hamer accepted.[4] As student Henry Winter Davis of Alexandria, Virginia, noted, "The duel was the only soap for a tarnished honor."[5] The two men, both around nineteen or twenty years old, agreed to meet outside Charlottesville at a place called Old Point. One of the key rules of a proper duel was that it be a fair fight, so Wigfall, an expert pistol shot, agreed, in accordance with the *code duello*, to use rifles.

Wigfall, who would later achieve some fame as a southern secessionist hothead and general in the Confederate army, embraced dueling as a path to glory. One of his classmates, Charles Ellis of Richmond, recalled him as a bit of a blowhard but nevertheless sincere in his desire to fight. Wigfall, Ellis wrote in his diary, had told others "that his father and brother had been each shot in a duel and it was his wish to die thus also."[6] Though duels were often found out and those involved arrested (ten students were expelled, for instance, for a rash of proposed duels in 1840, according to school records), this duel seemed destined to happen because the two students seemed so determined to kill each other. Just two months earlier, the two antagonists had plotted an identical duel, with rifles on rests, but had been discovered. University authorities were relieved not only to have rescued the two students from injury or death but also to have saved the university's reputation, so critical for continued state support. The duel would have proven "highly injurious" to the school, Bonnycastle noted in the daily journal that all chairmen kept.[7]

This second attempt at a duel by the two even more determined students—who this time had considered traveling as far as Washington—must have exasperated Bonnycastle and his colleagues. Student John Cheves, Wigfall's fellow South Carolinian, agreed to serve as Wigfall's second, taking on the tasks of handling the weapons, choosing a neutral location, and ensuring an impartial contest. Bonnycastle caught wind that a duel was in the works between the two foes, and he told the proctor to obtain warrants for their arrest. University officials learned that Hamer was holed up in a tavern twelve miles outside Charlottesville, so they dispatched the notoriously inept odd-jobber John Smith to arrest him. Hamer escaped. Later, authorities learned that Hamer had made his way to Richmond and that Wigfall and Cheves were riding out to meet him there. Determined to stop them, authorities sent a horseman in hot pursuit.

While students chattered about the dramatic manhunt unfolding in Richmond, they continued to deal with the pressures of their own prescribed daily routine. Student life, though violent at times, was also a gauntlet of vexatious regulations, lectures, and a routine ruled by the clock. Their straitjacket existence began with the clanging of the Rotunda bell at dawn. In their unceasing attempts to control the students, the Board of Visitors in July of 1827 had imposed an early-rising rule. Students were to be up and at their first lecture at 5:30 a.m. from late April to July. Previously, lectures had begun at 7:30 a.m. In July of 1828 the board made student life even more difficult: "The bell shall be rung every morning throughout the session, at dawn: The students shall rise at this signal & dress themselves without delay. Their room shall be cleaned and set in order, and they prepared for business, at sunrise; at which time, the Proctor shall, at least once a week, inspect their apartments."[8] Students detested the rule, especially after a night of carousing and the resultant hangovers. Janitors made random checks to roust students. Students constantly overslept and were called before the faculty to explain their slugabed behavior. Archibald Henderson of North Carolina excused his indolence by claiming that the early rising caused a pain in his chest—just as it had when he was at Yale.[9] One student called the bell-ringing unjustifiable and impertinent. A hoary anecdote told by one advocate of the Early Rising Law to cajole students was that "a little boy of his acquaintance had found a bag of money by being out in time to 'scent the morning air.'" Students responded by noting that the man who lost the bag was up even earlier.[10] The despised rule created a resentment that would build throughout the years.

The students awoke to cold rooms, sometimes murky with fireplace smoke or wet from leaking roofs, new but badly constructed. The students dressed in the dim flicker of candlelight. While the young scholars groused, the black slaves, always euphemistically referred to in university records as servants, fetched water and towels for each student to wash himself. The slaves also made the beds, swept the rooms, emptied the chamber pots, removed fireplace ashes, cleaned the candlesticks, and polished students' shoes. At times the rooms were so cold the students slept in their shoes or carried their bedding to sleep on the floor by the fireplace, dirtying the sheets, which slaves then had to wash. The dorm rooms were austere and cell-like—only 170 square feet—and sometimes shared by two students. Each room had one window and one door, and students used both as exits and entrances. The rooms typically contained a wooden table, two chairs, a washstand, a water pitcher and basin, a mirror, and a bed. A pair of tongs, andirons, and a shovel stood by the fireplace. Chamber pots were usually stowed under the bed.

Students' attire was an ongoing source of discord. Students in the early years of the university were forced to wear uniforms, capped with a hat "round & black."[11] In December of 1826—in yet another round of rule making—the governing board prescribed in excruciating detail what had to be worn:

> The dress of the students, wherever resident, shall be uniform and plain. The coat, waistcoat & pantaloons, of cloth of a dark gray mixture, at a price not exceeding $6 per yard. The coat shall be single breasted; with a standing cape, & skirts of a moderate length with pocket flaps. The waistcoat shall be single breasted, with a standing collar; and the pantaloons, of the usual form. The buttons of each garment to be flat, and covered with the same cloth. The pantaloons & waistcoat of this dress may vary with the season; the latter of which, when required by the season, may be of white; the former of light brown cotton or linen. Shoes, with black gaiters in cold weather, and white stockings in [warm] weather,—and in no case boots—shall be worn by them. The neck-cloth shall be plain black, in the cold; white, in the warm season.[12]

The rules demanded that students wear the austere uniform outside the precincts. Within the precincts the uniform was to be worn on Sunday, during examinations, and at "public exhibitions."[13] At all other times, within the precincts, they could wear "a plain black gown, or a cheap frock-coat."[14] The students, among them rich fops and fashion plates, bristled at the dullness of the uniform. The Visitors' motive in imposing the dress code was twofold. Students could be easily identified as students outside the precincts, allowing authorities to keep a closer eye on them, and perhaps more important, the required attire would disguise just how rich many of the students really were. The plain dress, the visitors felt, would help fend off continuing criticism that the university was the most expensive school in America and served only the wealthy.

The extravagant fashions of the students were an easy target for critics. So alarmed were the Visitors by the students' free-spending ways, they enacted a rule limiting clothing expenses to one hundred dollars per school year and, frustrated by the "indulgence on the part of parents," begged fathers to stop sending money.[15] The young peacocks would not be deterred. Even Poe, who was one of the poorer students, insisted on striped pantaloons and a beautiful coat. They constantly ignored the dress code, concocting fantastic excuses, some saying they were too poor to have their uniform pants patched and that tailors had lost uniforms. Others said the uniforms were too unfashionable for polite company.

Student Robert Lewis Dabney of Louisa County, Virginia, was aghast when he saw the way his classmates attired themselves. He wrote to his mother of the "extravagant manner" of his fellow students:

> I will give you a list of the part of one of their wardrobes, which I am acquainted with. Imprimis, prunella bootees, then straw-colored pantaloons, striped pink and blue silk vest, with a white or straw-colored ground, crimson merino cravat, with yellow spots on it, like the old-fashioned handkerchief, and white kid gloves (not always of the cleanest), coat of the finest cloth, and most dandified cut, and cloth cap, trimmed with rich fur. They do not think a coat wearable for more than two months, and as for pantaloons and vests, the number they consume is beyond calculation. These are the chaps to spend their $1,500 or $2,000 and learn about three cents worth of useful learning and enough rascality to ruin them forever.[16]

The students' desire for finery and the Visitors' insistence on plainness would ultimately lead to one of the biggest riots in the university's early years.

In addition to the burden of plain dress, students were also forced to eat plain food in the six "hotels" Jefferson had placed on the outer rows of dormitories. Hotelkeepers paid rent to the university and charged students for meals and other housekeeping duties. Students of all eras apparently have the same complaint about college food and its wretchedness. In fact, thirty of the fifty-two students assigned to eat at Mrs. Gray's hotel (on the southern extreme of the Western Range) were so disgusted with the daily fare, they petitioned the faculty for relief. In another incident involving Mr. Rose's hotel, students complained, "his coffee bad—his tea very bad and weak—has no vegetables now but rice—sometime ago greens but in very small quantities—Food dirty and filthy, frequently finds insects in it, particularly in bread."[17] Mrs. Gray was fined ten dollars by the faculty, Rose two dollars.

Another twenty-three students complained in a petition to the faculty of the food served at a Colonel Ward's hotel: "Whereas, we the residents of eastern Range, having with all Christian patience endured, until sufferance is no longer a virtue, the imposition of tough beef, spoilt bacon, rotten potatoes, shrinking cabbage, half cooked bread, muddy coffee, bitter tea and rancid butter, in consideration of our paying Twelve dollars and a half per month—and having waited in vain for a change for the better, think it ôur bounden duty, for the sake of justice and for the preservation of our health, to make a report of the aforesaid treatment of our Hotelkeeper, Col. Ward." The students asked the faculty to rebuke the wayward hotelkeeper.[18] Ellis, who dined at Mrs. Gray's, once complained that "the old Madame added a most villainous compound to our daily fare by her called Catsup."[19]

Hotelkeepers, for their part, complained that profit margins were too small to buy good food. The hotelkeeper George Spotswood grumbled that he could only afford to buy food fit for a "Yankee" accustomed to nothing more than "onions, potatoes and codfish."[20]

In theory, according to faculty rules, hotelkeepers were to serve meals that were plentiful and healthy, if monotonous. The faculty ordered the proctor to carry out surprise inspections of the meals.

Though hotelkeepers would occasionally turn a blind eye to the student gambling and drinking that occurred routinely in the dormitories, the sides often clashed. In one instance hotelkeeper Spotswood and a student, Thomas P. Hooe of Alexandria, Virginia, came to blows after Spotswood found dog excrement in Hooe's dorm room and ordered him to get rid of the dog.

"I have often spoken to you to send your dog away and if you do not my servant shall not clean up your room," Spotswood told Hooe, according to a remarkably detailed record of the confrontation. "I did not come here to clean after dogs."

"By God I'll flog him [the slave] if he don't" clean up the room, Hooe replied.

"You are mistaken you sha'nt do that."

"Begone out of the room."

"I will go when you request me as a gentleman."

Hooe repeated his demand several times. Spotswood stood fast.

"By G—— I will make you," Hooe said, bounding out of bed, putting on his "drawers," and shoving Spotswood toward the door.

"Say what you please but keep your hands off," Spotswood said. "I will not be ordered as a servant and will not go out until you ask me politely."

"By G—— I will kill you if you don't," Hooe said. He then seized a shovel and prepared to hit Spotswood.

"Make a sure blow or you are in danger."

"If you were not an elderly man I should soon show you."

"Your weakness protects you. My strength is double yours. You cannot intimidate me."

Hooe drew back the shovel as if to swing it and an excited Spotswood exclaimed, "Put down your shovel you puppy."

The insult was too much for Hooe. "G——D——! Do you call me puppy."

He then struck Spotswood several times with his fist. Spotswood shoved him onto the bed, where Hooe flailed his legs. Having subdued his attacker, Spotswood held him by the feet and said, "Don't be afraid I won't hurt you."

Spotswood then left the room and complained to Faculty Chairman Dunglison.[21] The faculty wrote Hooe's mother "to request her to remove him from the Institution."[22] Hooe then disappeared from school records, becoming the first and probably the last student to be expelled over an altercation involving dog excrement.

Not content to spar with hotelkeepers and each other, students sometimes brutalized the slaves who made the university run. In June 1828, student Thomas Jefferson Boyd of Albemarle County beat a slave so violently with a stick that it broke and blood ran freely from the slave's head. When hotelkeeper Warner Minor complained to the faculty chairman, Boyd expressed his "astonishment & indignation" that Minor would complain "for so trifling an affair as that of chastising a servant for his insolence."[23] Apparently Boyd had demanded butter from the slave and felt the slave muttered insolently. Boyd later turned on Minor for complaining, calling him a coward and saying, "If you ever cross my path you or I shall die." The faculty expressed its "high disapprobation" of Boyd but took no other action.[24]

But while students slept badly, ate poorly, fought constantly, lost their money at gambling, and woke with hangovers, the heaviest burden was attending class. Unlike any other university in America, Jefferson's school offered students the choice of a field of study. Students interested in modern languages, for example, would not be compelled to take natural philosophy. The students stayed in school only as long as they wanted. The school did not bestow diplomas. Attendance was essential—unlike at other schools—because professors were required to lecture, not just read from textbooks, an innovative method of teaching in America. Classes in each of the eight subjects lasted two hours and were held three days a week.

The students' exaggerated sense of self-importance—imbedded in their class upbringing—led them to act out in the classroom. They struck professors, walked out in the middle of lectures, chewed tobacco, scraped their feet, and otherwise acted like elementary-school boys.

Their energetic spirit led them to idolize and emulate writers like Lord Byron, famously described as "mad, bad, and dangerous to know." Students wanted to be like him. Byron was the most popular author among students, his books selling five times as many as any other author, including Shakespeare and Milton. Byron, an aristocratic rebel, appealed to their youthful sense of defiance. Second only to Byron was the poet Thomas Campbell, whose manly, warlike poems aroused the students' fighting spirit.

Thomas Tucker, of Brunswick County, Virginia, was one of the miscreants who made the lives of professors miserable. In April 1828, Tucker knocked Blaettermann's hat off after the professor accused him of making a disrespectful noise during class. "A noise is sometimes made in imitation of the drawing of a Cork from a bottle & pouring out the liquor," according to Blaettermann's complaint.[25]

But of all the bad behavior, university officials feared duels the most. A murdered student would bring unwanted attention to the students' widespread lawlessness and bad publicity to a university bent on protecting a fragile image as a quiet "academical village."

Aspiring duelists Wigfall and Hamer were the beneficiaries of the university's desire to shield the school's image. After dispatching a rider to Richmond to have the two fugitive students arrested, Faculty Chairman Bonnycastle learned from another student that the two no longer intended to duel but had fled Charlottesville only to escape indictment by a grand jury. The chairman asked the grand jury to let the matter drop. The grand jury refused. However, Bonnycastle persuaded a judge to leave the students' fate in the hands of university officials. The judge dismissed the case.

University records are unclear as to the fate of the students, but neither one returned to school the following year. Hamer went on to become a captain in the Confederate army, while Wigfall rose to the rank of brigadier general. Wigfall ultimately fulfilled his ambition of fighting a duel. He and his opponent, Preston Brooks, were both wounded. Brooks is known to history as the South Carolina congressman who brutally beat Massachusetts senator Charles Sumner in 1856, shattering his cane in the savage attack. At Fort Sumter, Wigfall was the officer sent in to demand the surrender of Union troops, and he would earn the title "father of conscription" during the Civil War.[26]

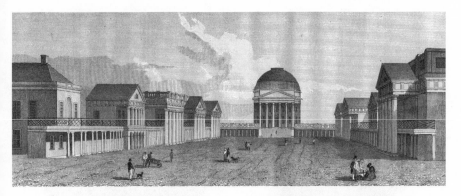

An 1831 rendering of the University of Virginia creates a peaceful scene at odds with the often turbulent reality. (Engraving by W. Goodacre, printed by Fenner Sears & Co., published by I. T. Hinton & Simpkin & Marshall, London, Dec. 1831; Special Collections, University of Virginia Library)

The father of the University of Virginia, Thomas Jefferson. (Engraving by Neagle after the 1816 painting by Otis; Special Collections, University of Virginia Library)

A view of the university from the east, showing the Rotunda as Jefferson built it, with no north portico, 1849. (P. S. Duval's Steam lith. Press, Philadelphia; Special Collections, University of Virginia Library)

Joseph C. Cabell, Jefferson's closest ally in creating and protecting the university. (Artist unknown, painting in Carr's Hill Dining Room; Special Collections, University of Virginia Library)

Professor Charles Bonnycastle was known for his acute shyness and mathematical acumen. (Artist unknown; Special Collections, University of Virginia Library)

Math professor Thomas H. Key was appalled by student violence, but nonetheless kicked a colleague during a contentious faculty meeting. (Artist unknown, ornamental mounting credits Terence Leigh; MSS 10300-a, Special Collections, University of Virginia Library)

Dr. Robley Dunglison, professor of medicine, also served as Jefferson's deathbed physician. (Artist unknown, ca. 1820; Special Collections, University of Virginia Library)

THE STUDENT

An artistic rendering of a university student by Porte Crayon, 1853. (Copy of original; Special Collections, University of Virginia Library)

A view of the Rotunda and Lawn from the vicinity of Vinegar Hill, to the east, ca. 1845. (Engraving; Betts Collection #18, Special Collections, University of Virginia Library)

John Hartwell Cocke, an original member of the university's Board of Visitors, staunchly supported the Uniform Law that students detested. (Daguerreotype, 1850, W. A. Retzer; Special Collections, University of Virginia Library)

As a student, Edgar Allan Poe witnessed, and wrote about, the vicious fights among students. (From an oil portrait by H. Inman, in the possession of Francis Howard, Esquire; Swan Electric Engraving Company; Special Collections, University of Virginia Library)

Gessner Harrison was the first University of Virginia student to become a professor there. (Engraving by A. B. Walter; RG-30/1/6.001, Special Collections, University of Virginia Library)

John P. Emmet, who taught chemistry, in 1825 became the first professor to be punched by a student. (From painting by Ford, 1840; Special Collections, University of Virginia Library)

A rare photograph of early university students, ca. 1850. (Tintype; MSS 6776, Special Collections, University of Virginia Library)

The Anatomical Theatre, rebuilt after an 1886 fire. (Betts Prints 1453 #39, RG-30/1/3.821, Special Collections, University of Virginia Library)

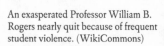

An exasperated Professor William B. Rogers nearly quit because of frequent student violence. (WikiCommons)

Law professor John B. Minor's religiosity improved the scandal-racked university's public image. (Ca. 1859; Special Collections, University of Virginia Library)

Professor Henry St. George Tucker became a much-needed moral compass for the university. (Artist unknown; RG 106, Special Collections, University of Virginia Library)

An ordained Presbyterian minister, William Holmes McGuffey was hired to teach moral philosophy at Jefferson's secular university. (Engraving by A. B. Walter, ca. 1859; from the Bohn album, MSS 9703-g, Special Collections, University of Virginia Library)

Chairman of the Faculty John A. G. Davis was fatally shot by a student in 1840. (Artist unknown, painting displayed at the Albemarle County Exhibit, University of Virginia Art Museum, April 1951; Special Collections, University of Virginia Library)

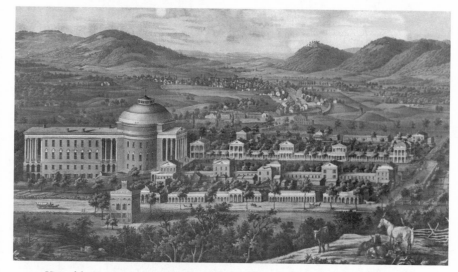

View of the University of Virginia, Charlottesville, and Monticello, taken from Lewis Mountain, 1856. (Edward Sachse, published by Casimir Bohn, Washington, D.C., and Richmond, Va.; Special Collections, University of Virginia Library)

The north face of the Rotunda, 1900, showing the Jefferson statue by Moses Ezekiel. (Special Collections, University of Virginia Library)

"Nervous Fever"

In 1827—the school's third year—professors and school leaders continued their efforts to control the students. Exasperated and oblivious to how students would react, the Board of Visitors imposed the "Uniform Law" that gave students another cause to rebel. Madison, now the rector, was the sole member of the board to oppose the measure, preferring instead that students wear a simple black gown as was done at Oxford and other European schools.

Meanwhile, so desperate was the school for more money to operate that Madison and the other Visitors agreed to borrow $20,000 from a private citizen. Madison had long felt that the state was too cheap when it came to supporting the university. "The hardheartedness of the Legislature towards what ought to be the favorite offspring of the State, is as reproachful as deplorable," he had complained to Jefferson in February 1826.[1] The legislature had done little to change his opinion since then.

Meanwhile, many students continued their wicked ways. They turned their dorm rooms into gaming establishments and whorehouses and the university into a vast saloon. Professor Key finally made good on his 1825 threat to resign, claiming the Piedmont climate was unhealthy. However, those who knew him thought the immaturity of the students drove him away. Jefferson's grandson-in-law Joseph Coolidge noted that the students' wild behavior made it extremely difficult to recruit professors. "There is not a man in America, who was competent to the place, who would accept it," he wrote to a brother-in-law.[2]

To outsiders, though, university officials kept up the pretense that the precincts were a sea of tranquility. "Our University is doing, tho' not as well as we [could] wish, as well as could be reasonably expected," Madison wrote to his old friend the marquis de Lafayette in February 1828. "An early laxity of discipline, had occasioned irregularities in the habits of the students which were rendering the Institution unpopular. To this evil an effectual remedy has been applied."[3]

Daily life at the university was a mishmash of tension and tomfoolery, scholarship and sin. In the spring of 1827, school leaders became alarmed at reports that prostitutes, some from as far away as Staunton and Lexington, were plying their ancient trade in Jefferson's hallowed school. Professors interrogated students, though the code of silence initially stymied the investigation. But professors eventually discovered the situation was worse than they had first thought.

Teenage student J. T. Wormeley of Fredericksburg, Virginia, confessed to keeping "a woman of pleasure" in his room. Wormeley said he tried to be "as private as he could be" with the prostitute, but other eager students had swarmed his room. She offered her services to those students when Wormeley accommodatingly stepped out.[4]

Wormeley also confessed to escorting two prostitutes from Charlottesville "by moon light." One remained in his room for two nights and one day. The two businesswomen had sex for money with at least twenty-six students under the noses of professors, hotelkeepers, and administrators. One of the prostitutes had even leapt out a dorm window when a professor unexpectedly dropped by.[5] Seeking to minimize his guilt, Wormeley claimed that prostitutes had been working at the university long before he sought their services.

While students tried to keep their gaming and whoring quiet inside the rooms, outside on the Lawn, the sound of whizzing bullets, bleating horns, and loud profanity echoed off the columns. A John Patten complained that a half dozen students, cursing all the while, beat and threw eggs at his doors, broke windows, smashed blinds, and shot up his house with pistols.

The professors tried in vain to channel the students' energy into extracurricular academics. For students willing to give speeches and write essays to commemorate Washington's birthday and the Fourth of July, professors drew up a list of approved topics. Among them were "The Life and character of Washington," "The character of the North American Indian," "The Principles of Grecian and Roman Colonization compared with those of Great Britain and her North American Colonies," and "Causes of the growth and prosperity of Virginia." In all, fourteen topics were posted on the Rotunda doors, which served as the school's bulletin board.

Professors also sent a chiding letter to the parents of students begging them to stop indulging their children with so much money. Students squandered their pocket cash on lavish clothes, on personal servants, and on sumptuous carryout meals from local taverns. Such profligacy reinforced the image of the school as a posh resort for students from prosperous families.

The students spent so freely that they ran up enormous debts with local merchants, professors complained to parents. The university, which had enemies aplenty, did not need the animus of local tradespeople as well. Professors in April 1828 urged parents to forbid their sons from borrowing and took matters into their own hands by barring students from carrying a debt of more than five dollars.

Intent on increasing surveillance, the professors created a scheme in which each of them was assigned a section of the campus to monitor students. That same month, the Board of Visitors authorized the proctor, the administrator charged with enforcing the growing number of rules, to fine students to reimburse hotelkeepers for the furniture the students periodically destroyed.

Madison wanted the public to know of the school's new tough policies. To that end, an anonymous writer to the pro-Jefferson newspaper, the *Richmond Enquirer*, described student life as an improbable paradise where students meekly accepted the new reign of law and order. The writer said he'd been doubtful that the sudden change from Jefferson's antipathy to discipline to the new board's embrace of restrictions would succeed. But after observing the students, he wrote, the university "is now in a fair way to become the proud ornament of our State."

"In its commencement, its police regulations were based upon too favorable an estimate of the moral virtues and studious habits of

Southern Youth," wrote the correspondent, who signed himself "Plebeian." This new, stricter school, he claimed, would fulfill Jefferson's dream of excellence and overcome the "prejudices of ignorance and the hostility of its rivals."

> I am disposed to attribute this circumstance to the new regulations by which idleness and dissipation have been almost entirely driven away. The exclusion from such an institution, of the young men, who rely more upon their fortune and family for distinction, than upon intellectual and moral worth; and who will neither study themselves nor permit others to do so, is not to be neglected. . . . The severity of some of the regulations is a little complained of as inconvenient; but acquiesced in by the young men from a sense of their advantage. The law which requires of each student, the surrender of all his available funds into the hands of the Proctor, to be paid out upon orders or drafts, operates as a powerful check upon the extravagance and indiscretion of youth. If parents would only cooperate with the spirit and intention of the regulation its advantages would be great.[6]

The obviously biased letter, as if written by a spin doctor in the university's employ, glossed over the steady flouting of the rules.

Meanwhile, board members continued with the ordinary business of the school. Robert Patterson was given Bonnycastle's job as professor of natural philosophy (Bonnycastle had taken Key's job as math professor). George Long became the second professor to resign. He accepted a job as Greek professor at the much more orderly and prestigious London University. Gessner Harrison from Harrisonburg, Virginia, became the first student to serve as a professor, taking Long's job. Harrison, a prodigy in ancient languages, was among the students who actually took their studies seriously, who preferred education over excess. Harrison and his brother, Edward, are the only two students known to have declined Jefferson's invitation to Sunday dinner at Monticello. The two wrote Jefferson that their father asked that they not indulge in entertainment on the Sabbath. Jefferson, touched by their filial piety, invited the brothers to a weekday dinner instead.

While the professors jockeyed for jobs, they looked for ways to tame the university and its expenses. When they discovered the school could no longer afford to subscribe to scientific journals, the professors agreed to pay for the critical subscriptions themselves. Meanwhile, students caroused. Their main, unrepentant diversion, day and night, weekday and weekend, was drinking alcohol to excess. They drank wine, peach brandy, "a stiff julep," spiked punch, champagne, whiskey, and brandy mixed with honey—anything to get what the students called "corned," or intoxicated.

The professors were no match for the furtive students, though they tried. In October 1828, they ordered the proctor to search out a "secret" barroom supposedly operating in the basement of a local tavern. Days later, the proctor nabbed several students at the bar, among them Thomas Turner of Fredericksburg. Interrogated by the faculty chairman, Turner averred that he couldn't recall saying "that he did not care what kind of drink it was, provided it was strong." Professors reprimanded him.[7]

Robert Wilkinson of New Orleans did not fare as well. For holding a "drinking party" in his room, he was dismissed.[8] However, after his fellow students pledged to keep him sober, the faculty relented and readmitted him.

While students partied with abandon, a new threat to the university's future swept into Charlottesville—disease. In August, the servants of Professor Dunglison became sick. Professor Emmet also reported that all of his servants were ill, noting that a great number of people seemed to be sick that season. Dunglison's wife had fled to Mary Randolph's house with her two "pretty children," leaving the doctor to deal with the emerging crisis, which Randolph diagnosed as measles, an illness that could then be deadly.[9]

Mary Randolph, one of Jefferson's granddaughters, wrote in August 1828 that the sickness had prevailed through the neighborhood all summer and had "generally been followed by dysentery & has terminated fatally in a great many cases. The mortality from this cause alone has been much greater than usual & as these things are always exaggerated by report . . . Charlottesville & its vicinity are considered by people not more than twenty or thirty miles distant, as the abodes of fever & disease & to be avoided as you would a pestilence."[10]

So deadly was the disease that travelers feared to pass through Charlottesville, according to Randolph, who noted that "there have been three deaths among the students at the University & these three have been magnified to such an extent, that it is thought the interest of the institution will be seriously affected thereby."[11] Had anyone been interested in checking on the health of the university, though, they would have found no record of the deaths in the official minutes, an omission that protected the school from criticism. Madison's annual report to the General Assembly on the state of the university, required by law, also failed to note that three students had died. (Though records are scarce, two of the students felled by measles in 1828 were apparently brothers, Patrick and William Aylett of King William County, Virginia. Another student, James Briggs of Jerusalem, Virginia, had died of measles the year before.)

However, as troublesome as measles were, worse was yet to come. A "nervous fever" arrived in the cold of winter in the waning days of 1828. And while it ravaged the university, surrounding neighborhoods remained unscathed. More than a dozen students took to their beds, stricken, and many others fled the precincts in terror.

The faculty determined that "an Epidemick had prevailed in the University since Christmas,"[12] though the chairman of the faculty didn't formally report its presence until a month later. Professor Dunglison told his fellow professors on January 22, 1829, that "a fever was prevalent among the students which might possibly be contagious." The professor identified the malady—also known as nervous fever—as typhoid.[13]

The diagnosis chilled the learned men. They knew nothing of how to cure the disease, which could be as fatal as malaria, smallpox, or yellow fever. The professors also apparently feared the fever could strike a fatal blow to the university itself, whose many virulent critics argued it had been built on an unhealthy site and should be shuttered. The university's supporters mourned the epidemic as a "public calamity" and feared the school would be "doomed by this visitation to sink into neglect."[14] The school—with a mere 131 students in its fourth year—had been trying to recruit more scholars, mailing out flyers to the capitals of all the southern states. Typhoid or rumors of typhoid would undercut that effort. And if news of the outbreak reached Richmond, where the General Assembly was in session, university officials could expect inquiries or, worse, criticism.

At the January 23 faculty meeting, a professor read off the names of those already infected: Aylett, Wilkinson, Morgan, Caperton, Haskins, Hubbard, Bentley, William Hunter, Robert Hunter, Trueheart, Brown, McLelland, Garrett, Carr, and Dangerfield—a total of fifteen students. By the beginning of March 1829, at least six students would be dead, according to Thomas Jefferson Randolph, Jefferson's grandson. The mortality rate, Randolph wrote, was nearly equal to that of the yellow fever outbreak in Philadelphia. Among the dead students were Laban Hoyle of North Carolina and William Hunter of Buckingham County, Virginia.

While keeping fellow professors abreast of the seriousness of the situation, Dunglison publicly declared that all was well. On the doors of the Rotunda, a note was posted stating that "Erroneous Impressions having gone abroad regarding the opinion of the Chairman on the existing state of salubrity of the University—the Students are informed that the Chairman sees no ground for alarm and they may rely, that should any cause arise, they or their guardians or both shall receive the earliest intimations of it." Though some students "called for leave to quit the university," they were told "there was no cause for alarm and that their request was discountenanced." Meanwhile, several of the hotelkeepers abandoned their posts.[15]

The ill students sweated and suffered with sustained fevers as high as 105 degrees. Some suffered bloody noses. Some found red "rose" spots—as with measles—on their chests and bellies, while their stomachs roiled with nausea. All suffered with general aches and pains, lethargy, and diarrhea. As the fever increased, the patients fell into a delirium, causing an agitation that gave the disease its nickname of nervous fever.

Overall, 10 percent of those stricken with typhoid in the nineteenth century died. Its cause—a bacillus named *salmonella typhi*—would not be known until well into the twentieth century, when researchers recognized that the disease is transmitted by food or water contaminated with feces or urine. Barnyards near a spring, cattle grazing and excreting in a pasture near a water source, or even flies that had swarmed privies or manure piles could spread the disease. The disease could also easily spread through unwashed hands when a person ill with typhoid prepared food—especially raw vegetables.

The shaken faculty responded to the typhoid threat by turning one of the university's vacant hotels into a hospital. They also instructed the proctor to "procure sufficient attendance upon" the sick students and hoped that the fever would disappear as mysteriously as it had appeared.[16] A little more than two weeks later, however, Dunglison reported that the fever still lurked in the precincts, noting that "two new cases of fever had recently broken out, one of which was of a most aggravated character, and that it was probably infectious, if Typhus Fever ever is so, and that moreover, some of the other cases had assumed a character by no means favorable."[17]

The already sick students were getting sicker, and more students were coming down with the fever. By early February, more than a third of the student body, forty-four students, had abandoned their studies and the school. The disease continued to claim victims, some described as being extremely sick, including a "recent case . . . more malignant in its appearance than any former case."[18] The fever's spread finally panicked the students. By late February 1829, twenty-one were listed as overcome with typhoid, and sixty-two students had fled the precincts or told the chairman they were leaving "under apprehensions which the Faculty cannot deem groundless."[19]

Word of the illness, meanwhile, had spread across the country. Josiah Quincy, the new president of Harvard, was interested in Jefferson's elective system and was on his way to Charlottesville when he heard of the typhoid outbreak. He turned around, contenting himself to write a letter to Madison in which he requested details of the innovative university's inner workings.

As students streamed away from the university, Dunglison worried that some of the "worst" students had left "under the pretence of sickness or the fear of being sick" and were spreading "an alarm throughout the Country highly calculated to injure the institution."[20] Still, despite what a temporary closure might mean for the university's reputation and enrollment, the professors saw no alternative than to shut the university down. They granted the remaining students leave to withdraw "for the purpose of avoiding the danger to which they may possibly be exposed by continuing in the university." The faculty suspended classes until March 1.[21]

Some students, however, had nowhere to go. Professors continued to informally teach them, while the proctor inspected the buildings and grounds in a blind attempt to eradicate the cause of the fever. Some suspected the disease emanated from the Anatomical Theatre, where students learned to dissect corpses. The facility, a large brick building that stood just west of the Rotunda, consisted of a spacious, airy dissecting room, a lecture hall, and an "Anatomical Museum."

Dunglison ordered the proctor to "remove every cause, if there be any, which can tend to produce disease; and for greater salubrity that he cause all the dormitories & Hotels to be thoroughly cleansed and whitewashed."[22] The massive cleaning effort couldn't hurt, but it wouldn't help either. In the early nineteenth century, the existence of germs was still unknown. Most medical doctors clung to a theory promoted by the "miasma" school, which taught that diseases came from bad air, atmospherics, or the vapors that rose from filth. They believed that emanations from marshes or any foulness could mix with the air and cause illness. Dunglison, the school's professor of medicine, who admitted his ignorance, nonetheless described the university's location as extraordinarily healthy. During his years at the school, he noted, "I never saw a case of intermittent, which could be presumed to have originated there."[23] "Intermittent" was Dunglison's word for malaria or ague.

In March, the *Richmond Enquirer* finally told its readers about the typhoid outbreak. The *Enquirer*, the mouthpiece of the Republican party under the editorship of the Jeffersonian apostle Thomas Ritchie, printed an article that defended university officials' handling of the crisis and lashed out at those who said the school's location was inherently unhealthy: "Is there any thing in the location of the University to which the existing malady is justly ascribable? . . . Nothing could be more felicitious than the location."[24]

Further down in the same article, William Wertenbaker, secretary to the university's Board of Visitors, put the number afflicted at twenty students plus seven others affiliated with the university. Of that total, Wertenbaker acknowledged, four had died. Everything, he assured readers, had been done to find the cause of the epidemic that had singled out the university. Still, he said, the faculty's "researches have been fruitless; they cannot discover the slightest evidence of any local origin, and their confidence in the general salubrity of the place continues undiminished."[25]

Eventually the epidemic subsided, and school life returned to normal. "There is very little sickness now within The precincts," proctor Arthur Spicer Brockenbrough wrote to board member Cocke on March 18, 1829.[26] To the full Board of Visitors, he offered a theory on the cause of the typhoid outbreak, blaming the way Jefferson designed the dormitories: "Very few of those young men (if any) have been accustomed to sleeping in rooms with the out door opening immediately upon them, which being thrown open early (by day light) of a cold morning, after having a hot fire the preceding night, on their being exposed to the external air it is reasonable to suppose they would take cold—and consequently be more liable to take any infectious disease." He also proposed an improvement to Jefferson's design—adding a floor to the hotels to use as a hospital for ailing students.[27]

However, critics seized on the death and suffering to castigate the school for its irreligion. An Episcopal minister invited to preach at the university shortly after the epidemic suggested that the typhoid was God's retribution.

Riot

In the aftermath of the suffering and death of fellow students and despite the admonitions of the clergy, students continued their unrepentant misbehavior. Faculty records from 1829 and the years that followed contain a long list of schoolboy recklessness. Though professors were long tired of their wards' chewing tobacco in class, insulting preachers, and wagering on cockfights, the students were not. They continued to casually smash the high-dollar Rotunda windows, sleep late, and ignore the much-hated Uniform Law of 1827.

Board members viewed the dull gray uniform as an easy way to identify wayward students in town, as well as a way to counter the image of the school as a place for elite, well-dressed planters' sons. But many students held dramatically different views. They chafed at the plainness of the uniform, which denied them a chance to show off their wealth and breeding to the young women at town balls and parties. Though the Uniform Law appeared to be just one of many rules, it created constant friction between students and the professors charged with enforcing the rule. Professors spied on students who sneaked off campus wearing their forbidden finery. The professor-student relationship had now devolved into the opposite of Jefferson's original vision.

The record books are full of uniform violations, excuses, and punishments. When caught without the gray dress, students claimed their uniforms had been lost at the tailor's, were too shabby to wear, or were undergoing repair. Professors chastised the students. Students, however, continued to ignore the Uniform Law. Left with little alternative,

the professors finally got tough; on May 18, 1831, they dismissed student
Robert Saunders of Williamsburg. Saunders, one of the first students,
had been studying at the university since 1825.

Saunders, called before the faculty for his continual violation of the
Uniform Law, was dismissed after reacting rudely to the professors. The
dismissal sparked a rebellion among students, for whom it was the last
straw. The angry students gathered that evening and worked themselves
into a frenzy over the expulsion of Saunders, a fixture at the university.
In the end they vowed to ignore the Uniform Law altogether. After
more thought, however, the agitated students decided to abandon "this
dangerous determination"[1] for a more forceful and cathartic course of
action: they would riot.

Rioting had a rich tradition at colleges in the United States in early
America. It gave students a new way to vent their frustrations. And the
public, in general, was surprisingly tolerant, perhaps because the nation
itself was founded on rebellion.

Though the riots had little success in righting perceived wrongs,
students had few if any other options. For instance, at William and
Mary in 1802, students rioted after professors punished two students
for dueling. The rioters broke the windows of every professor's dwelling except one and smashed the windows of the church and chapel,
ripped up Bibles and prayer books, and broke down a shop door. (Critics blamed President Jefferson for the disturbance, since he had gotten
rid of the school's professorship of divinity.) In 1807, Harvard exploded
with the notorious "Rotten Cabbage Rebellion." Bad food—fish and
rotten cabbage—sparked the riot that led to a yearlong campaign of
student resistance against the university. The protest included lighting
nocturnal fires in campus buildings. Harvard officials expelled twenty-
three students in the end, though eight were readmitted. That same year
at Princeton, students rioted after three classmates were suspended. The
rioters occupied Nassau Hall and set up barricades. When militiamen
tried to take back the building, students drove them off with broken
stairway banisters and rocks. Princeton officials won, but fifty-five students never returned to school.

Now rioting had come to the university at Charlottesville. Though this one proved smaller than riots that would later rock the school, it still scared school officials. The students, who had abandoned plans to ignore the hated Uniform Law, took to the Lawn. That night, after Saunders's dismissal, the faculty were still meeting in a pavilion when they heard the raucous noise of a mob of students—up to fifty, according to some accounts—blowing quills and tin horns and firing pistols. The students, wearing disguises, broke open the belfry door inside the Rotunda and began to wildly ring the college bell in open defiance. Chairman Patterson and Professors Tucker, Emmet, and John A. G. Davis, the professor of law since 1830, rushed out to the Rotunda's gymnasium on the building's eastern wing. But the professors were stopped by Saunders, who, with other students, urged them not to interfere lest "they meet with some violence."[2] Indeed the students began hurling rocks at their teachers, who immediately retreated to safety. An hour later, Patterson was sitting in his pavilion when he heard the crack of two pistol shots. The yip of a nearby dog told Patterson the second shot had struck the animal. Patterson jumped up and threw open a window but saw only a solitary figure running into the darkness. The mob continued its noisy rebellion until 11:00 p.m.

The following morning, a slave known as Lewis the Bell-Ringer, who had been purchased by the university for $580 in 1832 and would later be sold after years of service, gave Patterson the names of twenty students and three former students he said had taken part in the riot. Lewis identified Saunders as the mob's ringleader. Lewis said Saunders persuaded the other students to break into the belfry, "saying he would have his fill of ringing before he went away."[3]

Ten days later students attempted to reignite their protest, parading across the Lawn, lighting firecrackers, blowing horns, and shooting pistols. Other students refused to join in the rebellion. Still, calm would not return. On May 29, a dog was shot outside Patterson's garden wall. Another dog was shot at Professor Bonnycastle's that same night. The following night, disorder erupted briefly before petering out. News of the disturbances reached Richmond. The *Richmond Compiler* said several professors' houses were stoned by students. The disturbances changed nothing. The Uniform Law continued, Saunders was not reinstated, and the faculty punished no student. Saunders would go on to become a lawyer, a member of the Virginia legislature, and a professor at William and Mary College in Williamsburg.

Madison and the board, which met a few months later, in July, felt the professors acted too leniently. The board ordered the faculty chairman to record all reported offenses and their punishments in the journal. "The Board earnestly enjoin upon the Chairman, a mild and paternal yet firm and inflexible execution of the laws admitting to exemption from the operation of general laws, no excuse for their habitual disregard," the board declared. "And being indulgent to those violations only, which are casual and proceed from no design to offend. In this spirit the law respecting uniform and all the laws of the Institution will be constantly executed." The board further reacted to the disturbances by limiting the proctor's duties solely to police work.[4] Students were not cowed by the new one-man police force.

The students' riot possibly escaped wider public notice because one of the grisliest events in Virginia's history occurred in Southampton at the same time. All eyes turned to Saunders's native Tidewater. A slave, Nat Turner, known to other slaves as "the Prophet," led a revolt that terrified Virginia and the entire South's white population and led to even more cruel treatment of slaves, including those at the University of Virginia. Born in 1800, Turner worked on a plantation owned by Joseph Travis in Southampton County. A religious man who believed marks on his head and chest were signs from God, Turner often fasted, prayed, and read the Bible. He had run away from the plantation in 1825 but returned believing he was called by the Lord to lead his people to freedom. He waited and watched for a sign from God. He got it when a greenish-blue sun appeared in the sky in August of 1831.

Turner propped a ladder against the chimney of the Travis plantation home, entered, and unlocked the door for his fellow slaves. They axed to death Travis, his wife, and their three children. Throughout the night more slaves flocked to Turner, whom they saw as their Moses, and continued their butchery. The following morning, Turner and his followers murdered a Mrs. Waller and the ten children who had gathered at her home for school. By the end of the next morning fifty-seven whites lay dead.

This was the nightmare white, slave-owning Americans had long feared. Southern economies were built on slave labor, and even some northern states, despite the burgeoning abolitionist movement in the North, still kept slaves. In fact, slaves had helped build Jefferson's university and were responsible for keeping it running. According to the 1830 census, sixty-six slaves were attached to the eight professors' households. The slaves lived in the cellars of the stately pavilions. Some of the professors bought slaves once owned by Jefferson's relatives or Jefferson himself—the great proclaimer of equality. Even though the university was a marvel of forward thinking, slaves toiled at the school as if it were just another cotton plantation.

The white population exacted swift revenge for Turner's bloody uprising. Federal troops and the local militia joined residents in hunting down and killing at least 120 slaves. Bands of white volunteers patrolled the countryside in the weeks that followed, torturing any black suspected of joining the rebellion. Turner eluded his pursuers for more than two months before they captured and hanged him in November. His executioners later dissected his body.

The nation, Virginians, and students were aghast at the bloody uprising. Charlottesville's white leaders, mindful of the area's large black population, prepared for a possible slave revolt. But students at the university also continued their riotous lives as if the world—despite slave revolts—would never change. Protected by their code of silence, students did what they pleased with no fear of their classmates squealing to authorities. In October 1831, students broke the lock on Patterson's stable and cut off a horse's tail. Patterson was shocked by the cruelty but stymied once more by the code. "All the students whom I have seen or whose sentiments I have heard, speak with indignation of this outrage; yet I doubt whether there is one who would not screen the offender from punishment, were he known to him," Patterson wrote in the journal. "The discovery of offenses is the greatest difficulty in governing the institution, and, with the exciting feelings of *honour* among the students, it is insuperable. We are placed at their mercy."5

Students were so loyal to the code that even a daylight shooting was unsolvable. The day after the horse mutilation, a student fired a pistol in the room next to the office of the school's new police officer—the proctor.

"This outrage against the Head of our Police, was committed in broad day—yet the offender cannot be discovered," a frustrated Patterson wrote.[6] "The proctor mentioned to me that pistols were frequently fired, and, last night, rockets were lit off, in the western Range," Patterson wrote to the Board of Visitors in the journal. "He had used every exertion to discover the offenders; but, whenever any mischief of the kind is to be done, guards are set at every corner and, if an officer of the institution make his appearance, a cry of 'Look out fellows' passes, and the delinquents make their escape. I firmly believe that nothing can enable us to detect offenses of the kind, committed by a combination of students, but a system of *espionage* to which no *gentlemen* can submit."[7]

The students were clearly out of control, and the professors were reluctant to confront them. In February 1832, Patterson was at a party at a fellow professor's pavilion when students set off gunpowder outside. The professor refused to interfere, telling Patterson it would only make matters worse. The changes in the police department, the chairman noted, had done no good. "We are left as completely at the mercy of the students as ever we were," Patterson lamented.[8]

That same month, two Virginia students, George Pendleton and William Magruder, held the proctor down while a third, Andrew Hutching of Washington, DC, pulled a knife on him.

In April, students once again rioted. They broke into the belfry, rang the bell, fired pistols, and banged on professors' doors. The proctor complained it would have been dangerous to stop the students because they were armed with "heaps of stones and bricks."[9] In June, students broke into Professor Davis's stable and cut off the mane and tail of his horse. They then broke into the proctor's garden, pulled up his plants, and let his cows loose. Meanwhile, students amused themselves by shouting at passing stagecoaches and setting fire to their own outhouses.

The Board of Visitors had seen enough. The board members—

without Madison, who was ill—met in July 1832 intent on breaking the students' code of silence. The board ordered the faculty to initiate grand jury investigations against any student suspected of violating laws or knowing of others who did. This would force students to give testimony against classmates because grand juries had legal power to compel testimony. From now on, any student who tried to avoid going before the grand jury would be dismissed.

The following day, the board took even more draconian action, requiring students to snitch on each other or face punishment, including expulsion. The resolution, crafted by the board, required that students "state on their honor whether they know the perpetrators" of crimes. The board also proposed to ask the legislature to create a court at the university that could also compel testimony from students.[10] The court was never created. Still the changes were dramatic, constituting a fundamental abandonment of Jefferson's scheme of how his university and its students would be governed. Where Jefferson had envisioned a professor-student relationship resembling one of father and son, the Visitors had created a reform school where professors served as wardens and students were little more than inmates. And like inmates everywhere, the students continued to resist authority.

In the months following the Board of Visitors meeting, some students defiantly sang filthy "corn" songs learned from their plantation slaves, lay abed in violation of the Early Rising Law, continued to frequent taverns, ran up huge bills at the bars, and cast off their plain school uniforms to wear fashionable pantaloons and waistcoats about town. Even the simple demand that students tack their names to their dorm room doors went unheeded by many, leading to furious arguments between students and the proctor.

In November 1832 a gang of drunken students interrupted "divine services" at a Charlottesville church by standing outside it and singing corn songs. The sheriff's investigation led nowhere. The chairman of the faculty summoned students to his office to punish the blasphemers, and a grand jury began to investigate the incident.

One student, Hiram L. Opie Jr. of Charlestown, Virginia, appeared before the chairman of the faculty and asked to be dismissed temporarily until the grand jury had concluded its work. Opie told the chairman that "he knew some things to the disadvantage of some of his fellow students which he would not disclose." The chairman tried to discourage Opie but failed. Opie said he would "rather be dismissed than give information." Other students called into the office denied any knowledge.[11] Records do not say whether professors granted Opie's odd request.[12]

In December of 1832, in the dead of night, several students tried to "smoke" Tucker, the current chairman of the faculty, while he occupied his office on the Lawn. Smoking was a common prank in which students lit fires and tried to force smoke into the locked rooms of their classmates. The smoke forced the victims of the prank to run choking from their own rooms. In this instance the students tried to hold Tucker's door shut with a rope after lighting a paper funnel of "brimstone tobacco" under a colonnade near Tucker's office. Tucker forced the door open and pursued several students through the darkness of the east Lawn. Tucker called for the culprits to halt, and one did: William Ashe of Alabama. Tucker demanded the names of the other two students involved, but Ashe refused to give them up, in defiance of the new snitching law. The code of silence was inviolable.

The faculty dismissed Ashe the next day, but he did not leave the precincts quietly. That evening, he appeared in Tucker's study with a hickory cudgel. Ashe refused to sit, so Tucker, fearing an attack, remained standing as well. In his journal, Tucker wrote that Ashe accused him of being "the cause of his ruin" and that he was "desperate and he did not care what became of him." To Tucker, it appeared Ashe was looking for an excuse to beat him. After a tense conversation in which Tucker chose his words carefully, Ashe left with a harsh, parting insult: "I bid you farewell and by [God] damn you."[13]

One week after Ashe's dismissal, students attacked two wagoners. As the wagoners discovered, students could mobilize into violent mobs quickly at the whiff of any set-to. Wagoners John R. Miller and William McKewie of Rockbridge County said they set their dogs on some "singing and hallooing" passersby.[14] But perceiving they were "white persons," and students to boot, they apologized. However, the affronted students began to threaten them. Two other students joined in, and soon reinforcements of up to thirty more students arrived. The wagoners fled to the cellar of Keller's Confectionary (one of Charlottesville's best-known taverns and a frequent illicit haunt of students). A magistrate, a constable, and several other townsmen succeeded—barely—in persuading the students to let the wagoners go. The wagoners discovered, however, that the students had "severely whipped" their wagon boy and "chopped up" their saddles and harnesses, immobilizing their wagons.[15] Students eventually paid the wagoners twenty dollars each for the vandalism. There is no record the students were punished.

In the following months, students set fire to hay bales on the Lawn, danced and shouted around the resulting bonfire, fired pistols at the bathing house, banged a drum all night on the Lawn, and damaged furniture in the Rotunda by pounding it with sticks. One student tried to detonate a gunpowder bomb—twice—on Tucker's office windowsill. Tucker believed the bomb, if exploded, would have caused him "serious injury."[16] Tucker took the fight against student misbehavior to his classroom, "appealing to their better feelings to endeavor to induce them to take some active measures to discourage, if not prevent, the repetition of such outrages."[17] The effort had only mild success.

Students led by James Cabell of Nelson County, Virginia, adopted a resolution that denounced the recent attacks on professors as "unbecoming the character of gentlemen and men of honorable feelings"—but only if the acts were committed with malicious intent.[18]

Professors struggled to understand how to respond. What was mere youthful folly? What was dangerous criminal misconduct? In a letter to students, Tucker sought to define, perhaps more for himself than for the students, where that distinction lay:

> It is not always easy to draw the line between the venial excesses of youth and those which offend against the precepts of morality and honor; so that some who are merely to go to the verge of the line may unconsciously pass it—but two different attempts to explode as much gunpowder at the windows of the room in which I was sitting as must have blown it in, implied a disposition to mischief, or at least of

recklessness of consequences for which the indiscretion of youth can furnish no apology to one who is past the age of 16.

In short, bombing professors was crossing the line.[19]

Meanwhile professors wrestled with other administrative chores, some less routine than others. In April 1833, for instance, a corpse was discovered in a pond from which the university cut its ice. The corpse, described as an "anatomical subject," had been dropped into the pond by medical students.[20] The chairman ordered the proctor to burn the body. Students who lived near the Anatomical Theatre complained of the foul stench of the dissected corpses. The chairman also had to deal with routine complaints from students about too much cow dung on the Lawn, about filthy outhouses, about hogs under hotelkeepers' windows, and about the appearance of half-naked slave children loitering on the Lawn.

While students were vocal in their complaints, they remained tight-lipped when ordered to provide information on the illicit behavior of fellow students. Acknowledging defeat, the Board of Visitors in July 1833 quietly abandoned its snitching rule. There would be no compulsion to testify. Jefferson, in October 1825, following the first student unrest, had tried to reason with students, urging them to talk. The board in 1832 had attempted to compel student testimony. Now the board conceded the futility of the tactic, leaving the student code of silence intact.

Diary of a College Boy

Charles Ellis Jr. of Richmond enrolled at the University of Virginia in 1834, in the heart of its early, wild years, and the diary he left provides perhaps the only complete snapshot of daily student life—its tedium, its joys, its dangers, its burdens, and the perennial yearnings of youth for love and an adventurous life.[1] The diary recorded Ellis's second year at school in a three-month period from March 10, 1835, to June 25, 1835. The diary gives readers more than just a running account of violence and misbehavior. It details how students studied, with whom they associated, how they lived, and how they interacted in the social world.

While Ellis was safely tucked away in Jefferson's isolated "academical village," major changes were shaping the young America. The Baltimore and Ohio Railroad had recently opened, connecting the nation's western frontier to the eastern ports. Cyrus McCormick, in the nearby Shenandoah valley, had already improved the reaper designed by his father and patented his own, opening more land for planting wheat. Robert Fulton's steamboats chugged along the Mississippi River; twelve hundred steamboats were arriving in New Orleans every year, bringing goods that would tie the northern and southern markets together. Samuel Morse, meanwhile, was tinkering with a newfangled invention called the telegraph that would soon bind the growing nation even closer. Gold had been discovered in Georgia, prompting Congress to expel the Indians westward along the "Trail of Tears." Cotton, meanwhile, had become king. The nation's wealthiest men were cotton growers—and slaveholders.

This is the world that swirled around the university, its students, and Charles Ellis. In his own often amusing words, Ellis comes across as a typical college student, bemoaning his poor study habits, trying to placate the angry father who is paying his way, given to smoke and drink, slow to rise on school days, and constantly mooning over whichever young girl he has seen most recently. In his brief, 108-day diary, he finds space to mention more than three dozen young women, many of whom he unsuccessfully tried to woo.[2] (He would die a bachelor.)

The diary evokes the early university's commonplace life far better than the incomplete and sanitized records kept by the professors and the Board of Visitors, who were sensitive to any negative publicity. Ellis wrote honestly on subjects big and small.

He was derisive of the victuals served by the hotelkeepers, who were scrabbling for profits, not praise, from their young diners. On March 14, 1835, Ellis wrote, "This day made out to get to breakfast when the bell rung, something unusual; the breakfast not worth the trouble." Later that spring, on May 29, he again threw barbs at the hotelkeeper's fare: "College is no place for learning the Gastronimic art, and many is the time that I have risen from table with my hunger unsatisfied, but truly because I could not get anything eatable."

Ellis had a caustic sense of humor and enjoyed bestowing nicknames on those in authority. On the pleasant morning of March 26 he attended "old Blaet's Lecture, and found the old gentlemen in a fine humor; very witty, and making attempts at puns as usual." Blaet was, of course, George Blaettermann, the professor of modern languages, whose bulk apparently fascinated students. On May 7, Ellis wrote of Blaettermann:

> Had a most glowing description of Bonny's Party, at which, for the amusement of the gaping crowd, Old Blaet figured in a waltz with Miss Tutt, and to use one of Burwell's similes, he looked, no doubt, like a hogshead of Tobacco; hard to start, but once in motion, hard to stop, and moving on by his own weight, it being recollected that the honorable Professor, would, if our eyes may be the judges, weigh somewhere

near 3 or 4 hundred pounds, and Miss Virginia a light and airy form, she must have appeared like a fishing pole by the side of the Rotunda.

Bonny was the nickname for Professor Charles Bonnycastle.

Ellis thought exam day at the new University of Virginia was scarring enough to record for posterity. On May 26, at half past six, he "went into the Examination-room and after alternately scratching my pate and my paper for about six hours found myself the last man in the room, old Gess, singing and walking up and down and I writing like a millrat, a second copy of my translation, having finished it as early as almost any one in the class, but thro my confounded negligence made a mistake and had to write the whole over, to give in a fair copy." Old Gess was none other than Professor Gessner Harrison, who was almost as young as his students, despite the nickname.

When not describing classes, Ellis detailed his relish for parties, though he was rewarded only with nasty hangovers. A party on March 20 led him to write the next day that he "felt the effects of the last night's debauch most sensibly, a violent headache and nausea." Within two weeks, however, on April 2, he was back at it: "went into Lewis' room to drink wine, had a glorious frolik over a couple of Bottles, one Sherry other Madeira, great deal of noise, an uproar; came away at 2 with a severe headache."

Ellis was also a womanizer or, like many college students, aspired to be one, though with little success. After an April 14 visit to a young lady, he blamed his failure to woo her with his charm on a bigmouthed fellow student:

> Next paid a visit to Miss Mary Ella, where I found Sheppard and some one or two other men; soon got 'tete a tete' with her, and began to recal old times and former scenes when in popped Gretter and Mills to spoil my pleasure which had only lasted for about 15 minutes; after trying to make myself agreeable to all the other good folk, for Gretter is such a talker that no one can edge in a word when he is near, and waltzing a few times round the room and meeting Miss Walker here who came in whilst I was at Conway's, I cut out.

By May 10 his heart was swooning for a girl named Miss Mary, though there's no way of telling if the feeling was mutual. At this time, only she appeared to arouse his interest:

> As I sett up till nearly two o'clock last night at a Frolic given by Ogden, I did not rise at an early hour this morning; found the weather damp and chilly. Had some men in my room till after eleven when it was too late for Church, and so remained in my Dormitory till after Service, then went in to Hobson's room where I took a good nap till Dinner time; went down to Charlottesville, and attended Mr. Cobbs, saw divers girls, but as Miss Mary was not in town, and my foot was very painful, I did not accompany any of them home.

And, like many university students at that time, he visited a whorehouse—perhaps more out of curiosity than lust. But that May 12 expedition left him cold and disgusted: "Went in the evening with Harrison to the house of one of these common women, but found no inducement to proceed any farther, and indeed I can not see what pleasure any man can derive from embracing such filthy sluts as abound here, since he cannot even do that with[out] the danger of catching the Wildfire, a College name for gonorrhea."

Ellis's diary painted a self-portrait of an intelligent, somewhat self-absorbed young man who had grown a bit cynical. On March 28 he wrote: "In the evening spent a dull and uninteresting time at the [Jefferson] Society; too much etiquette and a disposition to browbeat every person who may not be of superior talents or impudent enough to overlook their sneers; perhaps 'tis better that such a spirit should exist in College; it gives one a foretaste of what he may expect in the world, but It represses the inclination for improvement which might otherwise break out."

Though Ellis reveled too much, on occasion he was also one of the students at the university interested in studying rather than being, as they said in his day, "a fine fellow." On April 8, he rose from bed

> early as usual, and after a walk, and breakfast attended Harrison's and Bonny's Lecture: then went down to Keller's with William Harrison of

Goochland [Virginia], a fine youth, but who is likely to fall a prey to dissipated companions, he has a high sense of honour, and a good temper, as well as good disposition, is not very quick, more, I think, from want of culture than any natural deficiency and he is now anxious to leave his present room for some more studious neighborhood, and if he applies himself, with his high connections, and superior advantages, may distinguish himself in after life, tho' much fear, he is more envious of being thought, what is here called, a fine fellow, than in improving his mind.

Ellis briefly scribbled his thoughts on campus violence, though he thought it too routine to waste his ink on. On April 11 he noted that "Warwick drew a dirk and stabbed Barton twice in the back, tho' not seriously." He also mentioned Poe and Poe's writing style after buying a magazine on April 23: "Picked up the last no. of [Southern Literary] Messenger, and saw a very fanciful piece by Edgar Poe."

Ellis did not write kindly of his alma mater's home. The merchants were too mercenary; the townsfolk were rubes. On March 30 he noted, "After attending Harrison's and old Bonny's Lecture, walked to Keller's, where I spent more than a prudent person would deem right; but a man can scarcely go to Charlottesville without coming back with a purse somewhat lighter than when he sett out." He added: "There is so much prejudice against the Students, among the county people, and citizens of Charlottesville that there would have been some disturbance between the Students and them if the trial had have gone against Oldham; the ignorant countrymen do, I verily believe, imagine us cannibals, or something worse, who can take up the bodies of dead persons, and cut them to pieces; thus it is that Superstition ever combats against Learning, and Science."

By May 30, just a few weeks before his diary ended, he added "mechanics"—a word for laborers—to his list of the town's faults. "Great commotion in college about a monkey show, to be exhibited in town tonight; all the students seem to be going down, and it is expected there will be a riot with the mechanics and other such ragamuffins, who always attend where there is noise and a crowd."

On June 1 he continued his observations about the coarseness of ev-

eryone but university students. The university, to Ellis, was the fabled
ivory tower that played host to the elite and well mannered; the surrounding landscape, by contrast, was a bastion of boorish behavior, ug-
liness, and squalor:

> Did not do much after Dinner, having promised Lucy Carter to attend
> her to the mighty circus now in town, which, together with a menag-
> erie now there, has taken nearly every student down to Charlottesville;
> at 5 started for town, and found it alive with people, this being like-
> wise courtday . . . was most infernally bored by the coarse vulgarity and
> wretched performance of both actors and horses; thoroughly disgusted
> with both audience and exhibition, I trudged up to the University, with
> Kelly, and a stiff Julep, which last came near having some effect on me,
> from my not having anything more substantial in my stomach, as I came
> away from College before supper, and did not stay long at the Dr.'s to
> get any.

Though Ellis's father was apparently footing the bill for his college
life, there was no gratitude expressed to the old man in his diary. On
April 24 he wrote that he

> was detained, by an invitation to a party at Dr. Carter's, from putting
> my intention of going to Charlottesville to procure a Hack and horses,
> and so what might have been done to-day has been put off 'till the last
> moment, and I shall probably miss a Lecture by it, which is to be much
> dreaded after the blowing up Father gave in his last letter, but it seems
> that whenever, he sends money he is privileged to tack on a long yarn
> of advice, I mean, that he probably thinks advice will be received with
> a better grace just at that time, and acts accordingly.

Jefferson extolled the virtues of the country over those of the city and
argued the point as one reason to build his school in Charlottesville. But
Ellis, like many students at the university, chafed at living on the bor-
ders of a small town surrounded by wilderness. "This day as monotonous as any other day in college," Ellis wrote simply on March 13.

Sometimes, his diary entries detailed the stuff of an ordinary day,
and in these entries, he opened a window on the lives of his fellow stu-

dents, capturing the routine of their shared existence at an experimental university in an isolated, hardscrabble town. "Rose pretty soon this
morning," he wrote on April 28, "and was rejoiced to find it had cleared
up; after Breakfast attended Blaet's Lecture and the Drill; next wrote
to Father, and after going with that to the P. office, and farther on to
Keller's, returned and read Tacitus with Burwell until one o'clock, when
he went to the office and I then spent the time 'till Dinner in reading
newspapers and entertaining some men in my room."

Two days later he noted for posterity the nickname for his dorm
room on the Lawn: "After Blaett's Lecture and the Drill prepared Harrison's Lecture for tomorrow, and at twelve, where I was most agreeably
surprised to see Uncle Powhatan drive up in the Lynchburg stage; went
down to Charlottesville with him, and after smoking a couple of segars
. . . wished him all manner of good wishes, and trudged back to my ten-
foot-box; read the *Mirror*, took a long nap, and rose time enough for
supper."

Ellis's diary also revealed that students kept pets, a violation of one
of the many rules imposed on the students. On May 2 he mentioned
that he had "bought a squirrl, which I am afraid will suffer through my
neglect." The diary's pages were silent on the squirrel's fate.

On May 31 he made another observation predicting consequences:
"We regaled ourselves with a quantity of strawberries, which I procured
from an old negro passing by; that fruit and cherries being very fluent in
college; no doubt Diarrhoea will be equally so in a few days."

Ellis, despite his complaints and sarcasm, apparently loved the university to some degree. He wrote eloquently of it on June 11, a few days
before he gave up his diary completely:

> Just before finishing my night's task was interrupted by the shouts of
> a froliking party who were cutting some capers thro' college; went out
> and enjoyed the beauty of the scene from the Lawn; the long range of
> white pillars, the open trellis-work, extending up to the Rotunda, and
> that building throwing its massy outlines clearly defined against the sky,
> lit up by a brilliant moon, southward the dark masses of wood present-
> ing a dark and gloomy aspect, and once more turning, before retiring to
> my Dormitory, up to the almost cloudless expanse of Heaven, studded

with stars, and a light gossamer cloud casting itself in wavring line for a few moments across the pure rays of the moon, like the veil of some heavenly beauty shading her lovely features from the gaze of man, then with a relenting hand slowly withdrawing it as if to exhibit how pure mortals must become e'er they can join the immortal choir above; quite practical for a fellow, who has been studying the changes of consonants and vowels for the last 5 hours.[3]

"Rebellion Rebellion!"

For nearly a decade, the professors and governing board of the university had labored to keep the students in check. Yet the mayhem continued unabated. After a decade of trying, the school's leaders still had not hit on the right formula to tame the wild teenagers in their midst.

Nighttime on the Lawn often remained a scene of drunken revelry. Students blew horns, fired pistols, and sang profane songs. When professors rolled out of their beds and left their pavilions to end the disturbances, more students would pour out of their dormitories, joining in the commotion or hiding those who were involved. A raucous, nocturnal affray that began with a half-dozen students easily mushroomed into a clamorous parade of dozens. Even some of the students began to complain about the constant nightly din.

In September 1833 the Board of Visitors—possibly at the suggestion of Professor Bonnycastle—devised yet another strategy to calm the campus. The Visitors adopted an order stating that whenever there was a "riot, or other serious violation of good order and decorum" on the precincts at night, the faculty chairman could "cause a signal to be given" for all students to return to their rooms and stay there until the morning. The Visitors suggested that the best signal would be the ringing of the Rotunda bell. Students caught outside their rooms after the bell was rung would be subject to any punishment, including expulsion, the faculty deemed appropriate.[1] The rule's intent was clear: students making noise on the Lawn at night would no longer be able to count on their fellow students to swell their ranks. But, as in previous efforts to bring order to the university, school officials ultimately buckled under pressure from students.

Professors did not tell students about this new restraint until November, when it suddenly became a flash point and cause of widespread alarm. During the first week of the month, Bonnycastle received a tip that students were plotting a "nullification" of the Uniform Law. Angry at professors for enforcing the rule so rigorously, some students had posted a notice headlined "Rebellion Rebellion!" on at least one of the school's pillars, and the notice called for a student meeting to be held in a dancing room to determine how to resist the "tyrannical conduct" of the faculty. Many students had signed their names to the notice.[2]

Bonnycastle responded by posting the new antiriot law—the one that imposed a curfew at the ringing of the Rotunda bell. Students' outrage at this latest attempt to curb their behavior caused them to suddenly forget their discontent with the Uniform Law. The antiriot law now became the target of their ire. To plot resistance against the faculty, they agreed to meet in one of the hotels. When Bonnycastle had the hotel doors locked, several smashed a door and entered anyway, letting more than sixty determined students pour in behind them. At the meeting, they resolved that the antiriot curfew was an ex post facto law that they did not need to obey.

The professors, whom Bonnycastle encouraged to stand firm in the face of the growing rebellion, reacted by targeting the students who broke into the hotel, singling three of them out for punishment, possibly dismissal. As usual, their fellow students rallied around to protect them. Douglas Cooper of Mississippi and John Jones of Pennsylvania notified the professors that sixty-eight students had vowed to leave the university if the faculty punished the three. Bonnycastle replied that "such an intention would not alter the course of the Faculty."[3]

The lines were drawn. Neither side would back down. At one point in the standoff, Bonnycastle, fearing the students would seize the Rotunda and thwart any attempt to ring the bell and impose curfew, considered a plan to put a bell by his pavilion. But the students met again. They appointed Thomas L. Preston of Washington County, Virginia, who would one day go on to become the university's rector, as head of a committee to address the professors. Preston told them the three students they had charged with breaking into the hotel were in fact innocent. Preston reiterated the students' view that they were not obligated to obey the antiriot law, and as for breaking into the hotel, they felt they had a right to meet there whenever they wanted. The students were ready to accept any punishment for their actions, Preston said, "let the consequences be what they may."[4]

After Preston and his committee colleagues left, the Reverend William Hammett, a chaplain who had recently been given permission to preach at the university, asked to speak. Hammett said the students were indeed agitated over the new antiriot rule, but most of them probably wanted to retreat from their position, if only they could do so with honor. The chaplain urged the professors not to punish the three students.

As it had before, the faculty backed down. Asserting that the three students they had intended to punish were no more guilty than any of the others, the professors censured the students and wrote letters to their parents but otherwise let the matter drop. They nevertheless informed the students that they would have to get faculty permission before holding any meeting on campus. "We do not conceive," responded the students in a rare concession, "that we have any right to break open any door in the University of Virginia."[5]

The antiriot rule, meanwhile, was almost forgotten. The Rotunda bell was never rung to quiet students, though the following July the Board of Visitors, now led by Cabell, Jefferson's old legislative ally, applauded the faculty for its course of action in quieting the rebellion. Still, the Visitors ordered the chairman to ring the bell only in the most serious circumstances and to rely upon the aid of the civil authorities when matters got out of hand.

For raucous students, then, nothing had changed. The hellions continued to drink at the local taverns (Keller's, mostly, according to school records), consorted with prostitutes, beat the hotelkeepers' slaves, and generally acted like spoiled despots. In one instance, three months after the rebellion over the antiriot law, Bonnycastle was forced to pull a gun on a student who refused to leave his pavilion. The student, John R. Jones, notorious for dueling and drinking, had come into the chairman's office loud and belligerent, as if looking to provoke Bonnycastle into a fight, the chairman noted in his journal.

Bonnycastle had placed "a stick and a cowhide within reach" before Jones walked in but ultimately could not rid himself of the upset student until he threatened "to shoot him if he did not leave the office."[6] Bonnycastle later explained to his fellow professors that the gun was not loaded. "I used the weapon," he said, "because it was at hand and afford[ed] the most expeditious means of ridding myself of a boasting and troublesome youth without the scandal of a personal scuffle with him."[7]

Avoiding scandal was a requisite of the professors' work. Just as the Board of Visitors tried to present the university in its best light to the General Assembly and the public, the professors worked hard to keep a lid on students' misdeeds. In one instance, for example, the school's janitor was ordered to quietly get rid of the various prostitutes who had taken to showing up at the university on Saturdays. Word of the prostitution, Bonnycastle suggested, "might injure the University."[8] The following month, February 1834, students grew restless over the dismissal of a classmate, sending the chairman an "insolent" resolution.[9] Bonnycastle at first refused to alter the punishment. But several weeks later, apparently facing the prospect of more student unrest and the possibility of bad publicity for the school, Bonnycastle agreed to soften the punishment, anticipating that it "would have a beneficial effect upon the majority of students."[10] That same month, a group of students gathered outside Bonnycastle's pavilion intent on breaking in and beating him. Law professor John A. G. Davis tipped Bonnycastle off to the plan, and the chairman loaded his pistols and waited for them in his study. Though a group of up to ten armed and masked students showed up, they knew that Bonnycastle was waiting for them, so they made no attempt to storm the pavilion. The chairman's preparedness to use force therefore kept the peace, and word of the intended assault never made it past the official journal.

But not everything that happened at the university could be hidden from the public, and the rebellion that rocked the school in 1836 made headlines across the nation, prompted the dismissal of seventy students, infuriated parents, and forced the school to justify its actions publicly in a "circular," a letter printed for wide distribution.

The cause of the riot centered on a student military company and the students' right to keep muskets on the precincts. From the university's beginning, Jefferson had planned for the students to receive military instruction, and in the earliest days they had formed themselves into companies and drilled. But the professors quickly made participation voluntary, and since the military instructor's pay came solely from contributions from the students themselves, he had left the university by 1831. The faculty named the proctor—at the time John Carr—as military instructor, hoping that the position would "accustom the students to an obedience to his commands, and [would] give him a control over them that may prove very important in promoting the general discipline of the institution."[11] In practical terms, though, the proctor played no role in the military company, and his title became honorary.

In late 1832, the faculty began allowing the students to run the company themselves, under the conditions that the muskets to be delivered to the military instructor must be surrendered whenever required by the faculty; that the muskets were to be used solely for military exercises; that the students agreed that, while armed, they would never violate any university rules; and that they must never fire the muskets within the precincts without permission from the faculty chairman.

The students agreed and formed themselves into a company called the University Volunteers. They used the one hundred muskets the General Assembly had previously given to the school, returning them after use to the Charlottesville jailer for safekeeping in the local armory. The student soldiers paraded and drilled, fired the muskets, and like the other students, drank and partied. Though the student company professed to be training for combat, its one annual mission seemed to be to escort the student orator chosen to deliver the Fourth of July speech at the Episcopal Church in Charlottesville. The student escorted by the military guard in 1833 was Richard Parker of Norfolk, who in 1859 served as the judge who tried abolitionist John Brown in Charlestown, Virginia. The students that year asked for permission to fire a volley on the Lawn to honor the day and were given the go-ahead. But soon the sound of random musket shots was echoing off the university walls. The angry professors concluded that "unless they behaved better they should be disbanded."[12]

The following session, Professor Emmet tried to make good on the threat, but the other professors by then had cooled down. They agreed the military company could remain as long as the students agreed to follow university rules, returned their muskets at the end of the session, and recognized the faculty's right to dissolve the corps.

But near the beginning of the 1836–1837 session, the agreement began to unravel. In late September or early October of 1836, the company consisted of seventy-two students, and, unlike in previous years, they began to parade and drill with muskets but without the required permission from the faculty. For some reason, the students never bothered to ask for it. Professor Davis, now chairman, finally noticed the military maneuvers after two weeks had passed, and he reiterated the terms under which the students were allowed to act as a military company. The students ignored Davis. Davis called the company's captain, Thomas H. Morris of Baltimore, to appear before the faculty. Morris did, and he astonished the professors by proclaiming that the military company neither agreed nor disagreed with the terms laid down by the faculty. The University Volunteers, Morris said bluntly, needed neither the university's sanction nor the professors' approval: it was, after all, a company of volunteers, and they "did not acknowledge the right of the faculty to proscribe to them terms of organization."[13]

After Morris left, the professors instructed Davis to inform the students in writing that they were not a legally recognized military company and that any student caught with a musket who did not immediately give it up would be regarded as violating the rule against keeping firearms in the precincts. The faculty adopted a resolution calling for the immediate removal of the muskets. Davis opposed the measure. He wrote in the chairman's journal that "considering the nature of students and the principles by which they are usually governed," the faculty action would likely "array the whole company in opposition to the Faculty, so that we should be compelled to dismiss them all."[14] Davis was uncannily accurate in his prediction.

In light of the faculty's demands, the company met and adopted their own resolution, making it as defiant as it could possibly be: "Resolved, That the company is not disbanded; that the company will attend and drill as usual, what the faculty may say to the contrary notwithstanding; that every member of the company pledge his honor to stand by his comrades, and that action of the faculty against one shall affect every individual."[15] The company handed a copy of the resolutions to Davis; it was signed by sixty-eight students. (Several members were unable to sign the document because they were under confinement, or "rustication," at a local tavern for drinking violations.)

This time, the faculty didn't back down. The professors sent the proctor out with a roster of company names to where the students were on parade. An officer of the company willingly called the roll, and every student on the roster but four was present, with a musket. Before the proctor left to inform the professors, he was given another resolution from the company to pass along to the faculty. A company officer bellowed, "Resolved, That we have our arms and intend to keep them." He then asked the members to vote "aye" by shouldering their muskets. Every student, all sixty-three in the formation, did.[16] No doubt the students felt themselves as noble and besieged as the defenders of the Alamo who had been slaughtered earlier that year by the army of Mexican general Santa Anna. The glorious deaths of William Travis, James Bowie, and Davy Crockett, rapidly becoming the stuff of legend, provided just the right kind of inspiration for the young hotheads at the university.

It was time for the professors to either put up or shut up. Unanimously, they voted to expel the rebellious students. The professors announced their decision at 4:00 p.m. on November 12, a Saturday, touching off two nights of violence that one of the later librarians, John Patton, called "excesses which have been unequalled, and which constitute a very dark page, in the history of the University."[17] In the darkness of the long weekend, students fired shots across the campus, smashed windows, rang the Rotunda bell without ceasing, battered doors, and heaved rocks and sticks at the professors' pavilions. "Our doors and windows were broken, our persons threatened, our families insulted by a drunken and infuriate mob," Professor Harrison wrote.[18]

The professors armed themselves.

"This morning about 6 o'clock, my family were awoke by the throwing of stones against the blinds of the chamber windows, beating with sticks against the front door, and firing muskets before the door," Davis wrote on Sunday. "During almost the whole day, there was considerable disorder, by firing, ringing the bell etc., in and about the University. Even during religious service, a party were on the Rotunda ringing the bell."[19]

Davis would later describe the "outrageous riot" as "a scene of unparalleled disorder and violence." "The acts committed during the nights of its continuance," he wrote, "particularly the second, were altogether different in their character from those which have usually distinguished college riots—they were the outrages of an infuriate mob. Our houses were attacked, the doors forced, and the blinds and windows broken. And there is reason to believe that not content with this, they contemplated proceeding to the desperate extremity of entering our houses for the purpose of attempting personal violence."[20]

Two members of the Board of Visitors, Thomas Jefferson Randolph (Jefferson's grandson) and William C. Rives, met with students and told them their persistent hostility was hurting any chance they had of overturning the faculty's decision. But the students would not be dissuaded. Two of the dismissed members of the military company, Richard Carter of Aldie, Virginia, and Cary Cocke of Bremo, Virginia, told Davis that "far greater outrages would be committed by the dismissed students" unless the executive committee of the Board of Visitors took the appropriate action.[21]

The professors were carrying pistols "for the defence of themselves and their families," Davis noted the following Monday, adding that the university buildings were also in "considerable danger."[22] The uncertain outcome of riots was always to be feared in early America, a circumstance that Davis no doubt kept in mind. Just a year earlier, in Vicksburg, Mississippi, a mob of several hundred citizens had stormed the city's gambling houses, seized five gamblers, and summarily executed them. In the end, Davis called for help. He dashed off letters to two justices of the peace and a deputy sheriff imploring them to come to the university's aid. They did. Armed soldiers were stationed at the Rotunda and throughout the precincts, and a grand jury was hastily convened to begin an investigation. Students began fleeing the university in droves.

A week after the inception of the riot, on November 19, the students gathered at the Rotunda and unanimously passed a resolution that stated the whole misunderstanding should be taken up by the Board of Visitors "or by an enlightened and impartial public opinion."[23] If it turned out that the faculty did indeed have the right to disband the company, the students said, its members would acquiesce. Until then no muskets would be fired at the university.

But the riot had already become a public relations nightmare for the school. Newspapers throughout Virginia and beyond were writing about it. The natural philosophy professor William B. Rogers, who had taken his job the previous year, lamented that "from more than one quarter sentiments of approbation of the conduct of the students have been heard." Students published a circular letter explaining their version of events, casting themselves as heirs to the Revolutionary fervor that built the nation, and imploring the public to give them the benefit of the doubt. The students begged readers to remember that the professors, like other men, were "as apt from sudden ebullitions of anger to commit acts which in their calmer moments they must regret and would amend but for their egregious pride." At the same time, the circular concluded, the students were "free and independent men," with the right "to resist oppression."[24]

One student wrote to the *New York Star* that he and his classmates were "not aware that a single musket was fired" during the rioting and asked, "How then can the Faculty presume to say positively that muskets were fired when they had been informed by some members of the corps directly to the contrary."[25]

The students were making headway in their publicity campaign. The *Charlottesville Republican*, while minimizing the riot as a difference of opinion over university rules, generally approved of the students' behavior. "This little controversy is the more unpleasant," according to the newspaper, "because the students have behaved generally with great propriety, both as to discipline and attention to their studies, for this and several previous sessions, and the University never enjoyed such bright prospects."[26] The *Fredericksburg Arena* downplayed the importance of the riot. And while the newspaper concluded the professors were right to dismiss the students, it also attempted to justify their behavior. The students' conduct, the newspaper argued, "seems to have been, in the first place, the result of misapprehension of their rights in the premises, and ignorance, or misconstruction, of the University statues."[27]

But with the students' November 19 resolution on the table, Davis sensed that peace with honor was within grasp. He proposed a faculty resolution that would allow the dismissed students to return. Davis's resolution noted that students, though misguided, might have been sincere in their belief that the military company was not subject to university rule. But a majority of professors refused to go along. Emmet proposed that only those students who disclaimed any participation in the riots should be allowed to return. Knowing that few if any students could return under Emmet's proposal, Davis amended it, adding that if students could not disclaim participation, they could still reenter if they were willing to make "proper atonement." The faculty adopted the proposal on November 22.[28]

Where newspapers had previously condemned the professors for acting too harshly, the faculty now felt the sting from newspapers claiming they had capitulated too easily in readmitting the students. The faculty felt compelled to respond. In a circular titled "Exposition of the Proceedings of the Faculty of the University of Virginia in Relation to the Recent Disturbances" and addressed "To the Public," Davis sought to justify the school's first mass dismissal of students and their subsequent readmittance. The issue, he wrote, was not the violence but the disobedience to university rules. With students now willing to acquiesce, he wrote, the matter was behind the university.

School records do not indicate how many of the dismissed students chose to return. Dismissal required Board of Visitors approval, and since the dismissals never made it as far as the board, the faculty chairman did not bother to write down the names of the returning students. Meanwhile, Patton later noted, "a sentiment adverse to the institution became rather general."[29] Whatever reputation the university had earned in the past decade had been tarnished. And while state officials had not gotten involved or threatened to shut down the school in the wake of the riots, the General Assembly would not forget the violence.

"His Only Motive
Was to Have a Little Fun"

The Board of Visitors, stung by the humiliating publicity surrounding the 1836 riot, met in August 1837 to reiterate that any student military company would be under faculty control. Furthermore, the board asserted, a military company could be "abolished at the pleasure of the Faculty" at any time. The board didn't stop there. In a sweeping new round of rule writing, the board sought to extend its control over the most picayune aspects of college life. The board forbade the students from bringing horses, hacks, or carriages onto the precincts; barred all student orations; and refused to pay any bills due to merchants who sold liquor. The board also berated university officials: the proctor was ordered to report all offenses he had seen, even those at which professors were present; the hotelkeepers were told to stop raising hogs in the precincts; and the professors were ordered to strictly enforce the Uniform Law.[1]

The need to write these rules must have been exasperating, if not infuriating, for board members, some of whom had been on the board since the school's inception. Board members such as Madison, Cabell, Johnson, and Cocke had failed for more than a decade in their efforts to find the formula that would bring order out of chaos. They had tightened and loosened regulations, then tightened and loosened them again. But the students' sense of honor, combined with their code of silence, their sense of entitlement, and the natural exuberance of youth, undermined the board's efforts. Nothing the board did seemed to work.

In 1830 the Visitors had adopted a rule requiring punishment of not only offenders but any student who aided and abetted them. The following year the board demanded that the chairman tell them every year about every single student offense, the name of the person who reported the offense, and the punishment meted out. In 1832, they ordered the students to inform on each other. That same year, the board ordered the students to testify when summoned by the grand jury, forbade them from assembling in the library in the Rotunda, and in a move that gave professors wider authority, allowed them to refuse a student entry the following year if the student's continued presence was deemed to be an "injury" to the institution. In 1833, they passed the riot curfew. The next year, angry at students' disappearance from the school during Christmas, the board insisted the professors continue lecturing, with or without them in the classroom—Jefferson's rule against a vacation during Christmastime must be kept. The same year, they threatened to dismiss any student who insulted a hotelkeeper. In 1835, increasingly alarmed at the number of students packing pistols, the board passed a law that even possessing a firearm could lead to expulsion. In 1836, they scolded professors for allowing students to go home at Christmastime and tiredly told them yet again to enforce the Uniform Law.

But the board's rule-writing resolve was frequently followed by remorse. In 1830, for instance, the board told professors to be bold in stopping offenses but cautioned them to respect the students' status as gentlemen. In 1832, the board failed to follow through on plans to gain state approval for its own court. In 1833, board members repealed the act requiring students to testify against each other and also advised the chairman to be less stringent in enforcing rules. In 1834, they abandoned the riot curfew law and softened the Uniform Law to allow students to wear nonuniform vests and pantaloons—though only within the bounds of the precincts.

While the board vacillated, the professors labored in the trenches, fighting their daily war against many students' academic apathy, disregard for rules, idiotic drunkenness, and everyday violence. Where was Jefferson's vision of faculty and students relating to each other as fathers and sons? It had evaporated. Professors found themselves acting—sometimes fearfully—as police, judge, and jury.

With the school now in its thirteenth year, many of the students of 1837 were acting as wildly as the students of the first year. They preferred whiskey to William Shakespeare, fighting to philosophy, cards to chemistry, and a dapper appearance to the drab dress code.

That damned dress code.

Despite their vaunted sense of honor, students intent on displaying their shiny boots, bright buckles, and the expensive cut of their clothing had no qualms about contemptuously tossing aside the uniform. Professors easily dismissed as lies the excuses students offered. For example, student C. H. Drew of Richmond claimed he had "purchased his pantaloons in a dark room" and thought they were within regulations.[2] A. C. Leigh of Amelia County, Virginia, averred that the merchant who sold him his pantaloons assured him they met university standards. Walter Nangle of Richmond said his uniform was "burnt by the carelessness of a servant."[3] Leroy Anderson of Alabama, charged with failing to wear his uniform vest outdoors, claimed he "walked out accidently."[4]

Though students chafed at the uniform, it was an important part of the Board of Visitors' campaign to deflate criticism that Jefferson's school was for the rich, extravagant, and indolent. Students who wasted their money on finery struck the public as fops. Public support and the money it meant were critical to the existence of the young university. The General Assembly held the same view. In late 1837, the legislative Committee of Schools and Colleges concluded that the state's five hundred university and college students had a collective debt of $100,000 (about $1.8 million today, or $3,600 per student). Legislators blamed students' frivolity. "A common subject of complaint in regard to our university and colleges is, that only the sons of the rich can be educated at them; that their expensiveness shuts them against all others," according to the committee report. "It cannot be denied that there is too much foundation for this complaint, and that the utility of these institutions is greatly limited and confined by this cause. But it will be apparent to any who will take the trouble to inquire, that the expensiveness complained of chiefly consists in the excess of expenditure beyond the necessary and proper expenses; which excess originating in credit can only be restrained by the suppression of that."[5]

Parents, who considered payment of debt a matter of honor, just as their sons supposedly did, were forced to pay off merchants. Students, knowing their fathers were bound by honor to pay creditors, felt free to run up debts. In its 1837–1838 session, the General Assembly made it illegal to give credit to any student in the state.

But the professors' pain in dealing with the violations of the Uniform Law paled in comparison to the unrelentingly sodden behavior of the liquor-loving students. Students continued to drink whiskey, juleps, wine with soda, champagne, and brandy. They drank in the dorm rooms, they drank on the road to and from town, and they drank in the taverns surrounding the university. Even when caught with a bottle in hand, the students were masters of the ready excuse. The bottle by their bedside had appeared mysteriously, the bottle in their pocket belonged to another, or some bizarre circumstance—a sudden drenching from rain or onset of illness—had compelled them to take a quaff of liquor. Nathaniel Burwell of Millwood, Virginia, accused of being stone drunk, explained that he had to drink a "bottle of spirits" to stay alive after falling through the ice of Maury's Pond while skating. The bottle, he added, belonged to another student who had asked him to carry it in his pocket, "which was a large one."[6] William Horner of Warrenton, Virginia, accused of drinking in his dorm, said the claret accidentally appeared in his room and was not his. However, since it was there, he figured he might as well drink it. T. A. Wilson of Georgia said he awoke to find a julep in his room and so "drank of it."[7] One student accused of taking part in a drunken revelry in a carriage was asked point-blank if he had been drinking. According to the school records, he replied that that was an unfair question.[8] Punishing students was difficult; students rarely implicated themselves and never their classmates.

Often the drunkenness begat violence. In April 1837, three students went into Charlottesville—one armed with a pistol he claimed to have borrowed for protection against town ruffians—got drunk at Keller's Tavern, and then returned to the room of John Baldwin of Staunton, Virginia, bringing liquor and the pistol with them. One of the drunken students, James Chapman of Orange Courthouse, Virginia, pulled the pistol. John Sheppard of Henrico County, Virginia, feeling himself in danger, attempted to wrest it from his drunken friend. But the gun went off, shooting F. W. Gilmer of Albemarle. Horner, who was in the room, told Faculty Chairman Davis that Chapman had "intended to shoot at the door."[9] Chapman was dismissed. Baldwin, who spent another year at the school, eventually became a member of the Board of Visitors, a legislator, and a colonel in the Confederate army. Gilmer survived his wound to become a physician at the University of Pennsylvania. Later that month, a drunken student was suspended after trying to smash his way into the house of a local "colored" woman; other students pushed a "drunken vagabond" into a room where professors were meeting.[10]

But students didn't need booze to misbehave or brawl. In December of 1837, William Whiting and Richard Jones tangled in a fight involving a shovel, a knife, and a chair. Whiting, of Cumberland County, Virginia, said the bigger Jones grabbed a shovel and used it to knock him down. Whiting pulled his knife. Jones stepped back but fell over a chair, which he then picked up to smash Whiting on the head. Whiting recovered, forcing Jones on his back, and during the tussle he said he accidently stabbed Jones. Jones, however, told the proctor that Whiting had stabbed him in the back. Whiting was scolded and told to turn over his knife. Three months later, an almost identical fight erupted. In March 1838, Alston Wright of Richmond stabbed another student who attacked him with a chair. Wright also escaped with an admonishment.[11]

Those were isolated examples of violence. However, one month later, violence on a much broader scale engulfed the university yet again. The riot was the fifth suffered by the university since its inception fourteen years earlier. The cause this time was Jefferson's birthday. Students wanted to have a Friday night ball on April 13 to celebrate the birthday of their school's founder, dead now a dozen years. Professors were leery of what might happen, given the students' behavior at a ball held the previous month. During the festivities, a student had nearly drunk himself "within an ace of perishing." "Both his physicians despaired of him for some hours," Professor Rogers noted.[12] The faculty refused to allow students to revel on Jefferson's birthday. Students responded in their preferred manner—with a riot. They lit up the Lawn with candles, donned masks, and loaded their pistols. Rogers felt they had singled him out for abuse because they somehow had learned of his adamant opposition to the party. "On the birthday night, tar-barrels were burned on the Lawn, the belfry broken open and the bell rung nearly all night," Rogers wrote to his brother Robert six days later. "Numerous students in disguise, with firearms, paraded the Lawn, assailed the doors and windows of some of the professors known to be unfriendly to the ball, and more particularly my own. At the same time the most insulting ribaldry was used, and their violence was such that neither I nor those in the house considered their persons safe. Accordingly we prepared ourselves with firearms."[13]

The next day, the professors met to discuss the riot. In the middle of the discussion, a student walked in and threatened Harrison, now the chairman of the faculty. The faculty took no action, hoping that student anger would fade. But the next night, April 15, the university experienced "another and worse scene of violence."[14]

"The dastards made a deliberate and almost silent attack upon my house, scarcely molesting anyone else," Rogers confided to his brother. "They broke in my front door, stoned my house on all sides, and for half-an-hour one of them amused themselves by breaking the glass of my back windows. The night was dark, and he skulked behind the wall, and it was impossible to watch or he would have been inevitably shot." Rogers blamed the code of silence for allowing this kind of behavior to continue. Though he would end up staying at the university until 1853, the violence prompted Rogers to tell his brother that he was ready to quit.[15] The university, he concluded, would not survive unless dramatic changes were made. Most students, he told his brother, abhorred the behavior of the miscreants, "but here is the evil,—their reprobation is not active, and it is only by being so that the institution can be saved. Our police is worthless; two or three rowdies can with impunity stone our dwellings, destroy our property, peril our lives, and take from us that quiet without which the situation is unworthy of a man of science."[16]

Following the by-now standard investigative procedure in which professors interrogated students and students refused to answer, a single student, Charles Hardwick of Georgia, was dismissed. Two others were suspended for a month for drinking on April 13, with the faculty lamenting that they could not link the two to the riot. But the riot of April 1838 was over, and once again students, with the exception of Hardwick, had escaped major punishment.

Despite years of shooting and knifing each other, of biting each other and swinging cudgels, canes, and chairs at each other, not a single student had been killed. And despite years of whizzing bullets, gunpowder bombs, and flying sticks and stones, and despite threats that prompted them to pull their own pistols, none of the professors had perished. That would soon change.

Caning, Whipping, Murder

Wayward students did not clash only with professors. Others had to be wary of the young hell-raisers. The students also scrapped with hotelkeepers over dirty linen and lousy food. They argued with local wagoners and laborers over their failure to show the proper respect to gentlemen. They tangled with local merchants over debts and the quality of their goods. They fought each other for the slightest reasons. And they bullied, beat, and abused slaves who had little protection by law and custom. They pummeled overworked slaves who failed to promptly light the morning fire in their dorm rooms. They kicked slaves who failed to respond quickly to orders. And they had no qualms about clubbing those who showed insolence.

The official records are short on detail on the university's reliance on slave labor, because slaves' lives were too inconsequential to note. But one university slave's beating created such a stir on campus and in Charlottesville that officials were forced to record the harrowing details at length in the faculty minutes.

On February 24, 1839, a "large and disorderly assemblage of negroes" had gathered near Littleford's shop outside the precincts to watch a fight between two black men.[1] Citizen Hezekiah Perry rushed up to the crowd and urged them to break up the affray. Two slaves attempted to carry out the order, but were stopped by a slave named Fielding, who belonged to Professor Bonnycastle. Fielding snatched a "stick" from one of the combatants and told the bystanders to back off. The two brawlers, Fielding said, were free men who had the right to fight.

At that moment, student Franklin English of South Carolina and a Benjamin Johnson arrived and attempted to break up the fight and disperse the crowd. Perry, in his testimony to the faculty inquest, said he heard Johnson shout, "Damn you, do you dare to push me." Perry said he didn't know the target of the curse but saw Fielding back up to a fence and Johnson come after him. Johnson "caught-up a stick" and began beating Fielding, Perry said. English joined in and "gave him several stripes with a switch and ordered him off." Fielding retreated fifteen to twenty yards, Perry recalled, before muttering something. English immediately pursued him, urging Johnson to lend a hand and accusing Fielding of picking up a stone. English whipped Fielding again.[2]

Another citizen who came upon the scene, Jesse Heeshill, said he saw the slave—now standing on the road between Wertenbaker's and McKennie's shops—holding a stone in his hand with which he threatened to strike English. The slave, Heeshill said, "was very insolent in manner and language," and Heeshill advised him to drop the stone. Johnson rushed up to help English and thrashed Fielding with a hickory cane. Another citizen, Calvin Jones, joined in, beating him repeatedly with his fists. Knocked to the ground and beaten further by Johnson, Fielding began to beg. His attackers relented and let him up. But Fielding once again ran off a bit and picked up a stone and voiced his defiance. He then took off running, with Johnson and English in pursuit. They caught him and beat him yet again. Again he begged mercy and was allowed to leave. But once more, the slave picked up a stone and the chase began anew. At this point, English asked student Madison McAfee of Mississippi to help him catch the wayward and now bloodied slave.[3]

Unexpected help came from student John Harrison of Richmond. Harrison was rolling by in a carriage full of his lady friends when he saw the chase. Pulling a dirk, Harrison leapt from the carriage and stopped Fielding at the very gates of the university, where the slave had apparently run to seek sanctuary. Fielding's antagonist tied him up and began to carry him toward town. The slave clutched the fence that then surrounded the university and said he would go no further because he feared "that they might kill him." The beating resumed. As a crowd gathered to watch the savage punishment, English and McAfee struggled to pry the stubborn slave from the fence.[4]

At the university, meanwhile, Bonnycastle had been alerted that some students "were murdering" his slave. Bonnycastle rushed out to the fence, where he found McAfee beating Fielding with a club. Bonnycastle seized McAfee by the collar, and the two exchanged heated words. Heeshill later told the investigating faculty that he heard McAfee tell Bonnycastle "that any man who would protect a negro as much in the wrong as Fielding is no better than a negro himself."[5] Bonnycastle recalled McAfee exclaiming "that if he interfered to protect his servant in his insolence, he was the greater rascal of the two."[6] McAfee also told the professor that "if he had done right," he should have knocked down Bonnycastle for grabbing him by the collar, the professor recalled.[7] English intervened and grabbed Bonnycastle, "holding him back" and trying to explain the situation.[8] McAfee returned to beating Fielding. Bonnycastle, meanwhile, urged his slave to "run and make his escape."[9] But Fielding was too exhausted and too severely injured to move with any speed and was quickly caught again. Johnson began beating him with a stick, and another student knocked the badly wounded slave to the ground. In a last bid at defiance, Fielding stood, grabbed McAfee's watch chain, and threw it to the ground. English, with one blow, knocked the slave down. "Fielding now humbled himself and English expressed himself satisfied," according to Heeshill's deposition to the faculty.[10]

Bonnycastle asked the faculty to investigate the ugly incident, not because a slave was nearly beaten to death, but because a professor had been disrespected. McAfee had threatened to whip Bonnycastle, according to one witness. In their defense, McAfee and English said they regretted their conduct toward Bonnycastle but excused themselves by stating that "he had thrown off the guard of a Professor and assumed (as they supposed) that of a man recklessly interposing to screen his servant from merited chastisement."[11] Another witness, meanwhile, Jefferson's youngest grandson, George Wythe Randolph of Albemarle, said that Fielding "provoked the new attacks upon him by his insolent conduct; but he saw the attack once renewed when the servant was not provoking it."[12] Randolph further said that Bonnycastle's method of interfering was "calculated to irritate" and that had the professor used a gentler approach, the students would not have turned on Bonnycastle.[13]

Despite Bonnycastle's complaint, the faculty unanimously decided "under the peculiar circumstance" of the case not to punish the students for the alleged disrespect toward Bonnycastle.[14] If there were a complaint to be made for the abuse of Fielding—Bonnycastle's property—it should be left up to the courts. The students, meanwhile, moved on with their hurly-burly lives. Harrison would be dismissed from the university the following month for inattentiveness and then disappear from history.[15] After closing out the inquiry, the faculty then moved to another investigation—a complaint by twenty-three students about the food at Colonel Ward's hotel.

The brutal beating of Fielding survives as one of the ugliest instances in the history of the young university. But less than a month later, a second beating occurred that, though less vicious, would create a public stir—this was the horsewhipping of chairman Gessner Harrison. Students Binford and Russell accosted Harrison as he left the Rotunda. The two students had been ordered off the university property by Harrison for "gross violations" of school rules.[16] The two came looking for revenge. While one held him, the other horsewhipped the young professor while students looked on. Professor Rogers called the act "another disgraceful outrage committed by students."[17]

"This ruffian deed took place in the presence of nearly 100 students, of whom only two or three attempted to interpose, and they not efficiently," Rogers wrote to his brother Henry. "The rest, though as they say strongly disapproving the outrage, looked on with folded arms!!"[18] The two students fled, were captured by a posse in a shoot-out, and jailed in Charlottesville. Russell was dangerously wounded, shot in the shoulder.

Students, to Rogers's mortification, rallied to the miscreants' side, threatening to break them out of jail. The student leaders tried to rally their classmates by parading Russell's bloody coat about the Lawn "to excite sympathy, and to inflame them against the officers and the Faculty," Rogers wrote.[19] Facing yet another student riot, the faculty capitulated and dropped charges against the two. The reaction of the students illustrates the mob loyalty that always cast others as the enemy and themselves as the oppressed.

The students could randomly shoot at passersby and expect no censure from fellow students. They could shoot dogs, beat slaves, whip professors, hole up with prostitutes, vandalize and scandalize the university, and settle arguments at the point of a knife and expect nothing but support and understanding from their fellow scholars. But could they murder and get away with it? That question would soon be answered.

One of the new traditions at the young university was the celebration of the 1836 military company riot, which the students had interpreted as a victory over professorial authority. Every November the students fired their pistols, set off firecrackers, lit fires, and in general spent the night caterwauling. The students treated the day as their own Fourth of July and Declaration of Independence combined, according to the early school historian Alexander Bruce. November 12, 1840, was no different. The ruckus was not unusual, however; just a few days earlier students had celebrated the election of William Henry Harrison to the presidency by burning tar barrels on the Lawn. With the students' encouragement, a professor had orated on the glory of the Whig victory.

But on this autumn night, the disturbance was too much for chairman Davis to bear. He stepped out, as he no doubt had many times in the past, to put a halt to the hullabaloo, which was caused predominately by two masked students parading around the Lawn firing blank cartridges.

John Anthony Gardner Davis had seen student mayhem both as a student and as a professor—he was a student in the university's inaugural class of 1825 and had been its law professor since 1830. Born and raised in Middlesex County, Virginia, he raised his own sons at the university, and three were now students. The youngest was no older than fourteen. Davis himself was thirty-eight years old.

Around 9:00 p.m., as Davis stepped out of his pavilion, he saw one of the masked students hiding behind one of the pillars. Davis jumped for him and reached to unmask the small, bothersome student. The student fled but turned after a few steps, pointed his pistol, and without uttering a word, fired at Davis's gut. The student had fired no blank cartridge. A bullet pierced Davis's abdomen, and he fell to the ground with a groan.

Students soon flocked to the pavilion as word spread that a professor had been shot. Several picked up Davis's limp, bleeding body and brought the wounded man inside. "The young men who carried him in say that the sight of Mrs. Davis and her sufferings was painful beyond conception, and produced emotions in themselves more intense than they had ever experienced," wrote student Robert Lewis Dabney of Louisa County, Virginia, to his brother. "Yet when we attempted to gain some information from him to enable us to identify the man, she prevented him, by her influence, from saying a word. Such is the heroic forgiveness of the Christian." Davis, however, did describe his assailant as short.[20]

And so began the search for the student who shot the professor. This time, the students joined in the hunt for one of their own, outraged at the assassin-like character of the attack. Where previous acts of violence had always ended with students closing ranks, this time—for the first time—they sided with university authorities and recognized that there were limits to their insubordinate behavior. They held a meeting the following morning to express their "indignation and abhorrence."[21]

While Davis lay dying, the search for the shooter began in earnest. Suspicion quickly fell on William Kincaid of South Carolina, whom students identified as one of the two pistol-firing revelers. A committee of students formed to find and interrogate Kincaid. "He acknowledged having been one of the rioters, denied the act, and refused to give any information as to the names, disguises or motives of the others," Dabney wrote on November 13. "As we had no legal authority we were obliged to release him and they very foolishly let him off, taking his word not to abscond."[22] To Dabney's disgust, Kincaid immediately ran off and was seen running through the fields adjacent to the university. The authorities were soon in hot pursuit of Kincaid. But back on campus, all short students were summoned to the Rotunda, where their classmates demanded that each one of them prove their innocence.

Newspapers, meanwhile, had learned of the shooting. Initial stories suggested the wound was not fatal. "We understand that Professor Davis of the University of Virginia was shot by an unknown hand, with a pistol, in front of his dwelling, on Thursday night about 9 o'clock," the *Richmond Enquirer* reported. "The individual who committed the act is said to have been masked at the time. The ball was received just below the navel, and is said to have passed around the abdomen down to the fleshy part of the thigh, without entering the cavity. It affords the numerous friends of Mr. Davis in this community infinite pleasure to learn that the wound is not considered mortal."[23]

But Davis was not getting better, and at sundown on November 14, a Saturday, he succumbed to his wounds. The public was stupefied. Under the headline "Horrible Outrage!" the *Enquirer* demanded justice: "In the name of humanity thus barbarously outraged, in the name of Virginia thus deprived of one of her most excellent citizens, in the name of the University thus stripped of one of her brightest ornaments, in the name of his family thus cut off from their beloved protector, we hail the determined spirit of the Students, and we call upon them, upon every friend of justice and civilization, to assist in the administration of the laws of the land."[24]

After Davis's death, surgeons finally extracted the bullet, which they had initially been unable to find because it had passed through the abdomen and groin, lodging below the hip bone. The bullet would lead the student investigators to the shooter.

A student quickly recognized the bullet as a misshapen lead ball he had loaned, with a pistol and blanks, to student Joseph Semmes of Washington, Georgia. At the same time, the concerned students had pieced together the suspects' movements that night; the two disguised students had passed by a group of other students who had warned them to be careful because "Davis was on the watch."[25]

"One of the two immediately walked down that way, loading his pistol; but, in addition to the former charge of powder, he was seen to put in a ball, ramming it down against the wall of the house as he went," Dabney recalled. "Nobody at that time, however, suspected anything, or felt himself authorized to interfere." Moments later, students heard the crack of a pistol and saw the masked student rushing off across the darkness of the Lawn.[26]

With the bullet implicating Semmes and authorities out searching for Kincaid, the responsibility of capturing Semmes fell to the outraged students. Bearing a warrant and expecting a violent confrontation, Dabney and a classmate found Semmes hiding in a pine grove and arrested him. He offered no resistance.

At the university, Davis's colleagues took his death hard, especially coming just weeks after the death of Professor Bonnycastle, one of the school's founding professors. Davis was thirty-eight. "This morning I assisted in laying another of my colleagues in the grave," wrote Professor Rogers. "My kind friend, and long my bosom companion, Davis, died on Saturday evening of a wound received on the preceding Thursday night! . . . He died a Christian hero, blessing his family and his weeping colleagues and friends assembled around his bedside." His pregnant widow, Mary Jane, was briefly "bereft of reason," Rogers said.[27] She would later miscarry, apparently because of the shock of her husband's murder.

Semmes, whom Rogers described as a "heartless though determined villain," was jailed in Charlottesville.[28] He remained there for months, awaiting trial. Shortly before the trial was to begin, he fell sick. Two important witnesses, meanwhile, absconded, according to Dabney. Semmes made use of powerful lawyers—the law firm of Leigh, Lyons, and Gilmer—who persuaded a court to set bail at $25,000. After the bond was posted—presumably by his wealthy family—Semmes disappeared. The following year, the university students learned that he had committed suicide at his home in Georgia. Davis's grave is marked by a tombstone at the university's graveyard, located within a short walk of the Lawn where he died. Bonnycastle was buried nearby.

The year had been one of the most tumultuous in the university's history. One professor had been murdered, and a second had died. A third, Professor Blaettermann, had been fired in disgrace for beating his wife in public. And yet by the end of the year, the school had apparently shifted dramatically for the better. The students had uncharacteristically worked alongside their long-standing antagonists—the professors. The murder had jolted them into taking responsible, mature action. Newspapers, and thus the public, had taken note. "The students to a man joined in the pursuit of the villains, and it was by their efforts they were secured," Rogers wrote to his brothers. "They have also been active in collecting the evidence, which, as it now exists, convicts the principal of murder in the first degree, probably. . . . The conduct and feelings of the students on this occasion have shown that they are entirely worthy of the high opinion the Faculty had formed of them."[29]

Though more riots, public anger, and legislative scrutiny loomed, the school seemed to be on its way to stability.

Henry St. George Tucker
and His "New" Old Strategy

America was changing. Railroads, steamboats, the telegraph—all were combining to transform the American landscape. The university was changing too. Following the loss of three professors in 1840—Bonnycastle to death, Davis to murder, and Blaettermann to scandal—Rector Chapman Johnson and the Board of Visitors moved to fill the crucial vacancies. As the new school year began, only five professors remained. Gessner Harrison continued to teach Greek and Latin. Emmet, the last professor left from the inaugural year, still taught chemistry. Tucker remained chair of moral philosophy. James L. Cabell, one of Virginia's Cabell clan, lectured in anatomy and surgery. And finally, Henry Howard was the medical professor, the third to fill the role since Robley Dunglison's departure in 1833.

Johnson was eager to fill the vacancies as quickly as possible because the number of professors affected the school's perpetually tenuous revenue stream as well as the size of student enrollment. Despite almost two decades in existence, the school still struggled to attract students. The class that entered in the opening year of 1825 peaked at 125 students. By 1840, the number had grown only to 179. The class that entered in 1841 numbered an even more dismal 170. Davis's murder had dampened enthusiasm for the school. University leaders believed too many people still unfairly considered the school a godless and violent enclave. Meanwhile, the new southern states, such as Alabama, had opened their own universities to compete with other long-standing southern universities in Georgia, North and South Carolina, and Tennessee. By 1842, the number of students entering Jefferson's university had plummeted to

128, the lowest number since the class of 1828–1829, the class that had been struck by typhoid. Incredibly, the 1842 enrollment was less than half of what it was in 1836, a mere six years earlier.

The school was so hard-pressed for money that Johnson and his fellow board members were forced to decline a proposal by the Society of Alumni to create a department of history and English literature. The state's support, never enthusiastic, had remained stagnant at $15,000 a year since 1819.

Looking to quickly improve the university's perilous situation, the Board of Visitors met in July 1841 to fill the three vacant posts. They hired J. J. Sylvester of University College, London, to teach math. Blaettermann's job in modern languages went to Charles Kraitser, a Hungarian whose Catholic religion caused some grumbling in Richmond. Both of these were one-year appointments. The hire that would prove most relevant to the university's immediate circumstances was the recruitment of the esteemed Henry St. George Tucker as professor of law. The board made the world-wise Tucker chairman immediately, replacing the still youthful Harrison. Tucker, in his early sixties, was the son of a U.S. district judge. Tucker himself was currently chief judge of the Virginia Court of Appeals. A graduate of William and Mary College, he had settled in Winchester, Virginia, at the age of twenty-two and begun practicing law. With the advent of the War of 1812, he enlisted as an officer. He served four years in the U.S. House of Representatives and another four years in the state senate. He served as the state chancellor before becoming an appeals judge.

Perhaps the board that hired him did not know that Tucker held Jeffersonian views on human nature and believed that appeals to honor and a sense of right were more effective than strict rules and punishment. That belief had led Jefferson to found a university with a uniquely lax disciplinary system. Jefferson believed students would govern themselves. "The insubordination of our youth is now the greatest obstacle to their education," Jefferson had written Ticknor, of Harvard, back in July 1823. "We may lessen the difficulty, perhaps, by avoiding too much government, by requiring no useless observances, none which shall multiply occasions for dissatisfaction, disobedience and revolt."[1]

Tucker held identical views. However, he entered an "academical village" that had been increasingly run along opposite lines. While en-rollment languished, rule making flourished.

Many of the students of 1841 behaved as abominably as Virginians had come to expect they would. Attending class seemed to be treated as an option. W. L. Anderson of Alabama skipped Greek and Latin class thirteen times during the month of January, faculty minutes show. Henry A. Sydnor of Pittsylvania County absented himself four times. In mathematics, William R. Galt of Norfolk, Virginia, failed to show up at class six times during the month. Other students were equally lax in attendance.

Students ignored their studies as well. In March's intermediate ex-ams, according to the faculty minutes, many students turned in blank sheets of paper. For example, seven students turned in "blanks" for math, and five medical students turned in "blanks" in the obstetrics exam. Others turned in scores so dismal that the faculty felt compelled to record them for posterity. J. G. Crouch of Richmond scored 10 out of 80 in junior Greek. Marcellus McKennie, who was born at the uni-versity, managed to correctly answer only 7 out of 80 in Greek. John R. Thompson of Richmond correctly answered a bare 5 out of 80.[2]

Meanwhile, students continued to drink heavily, brandish weap-ons, and chase women. In December 1841, Frederic Hall of Portsmouth got stinking drunk at Mrs. Gray's hotel, fired a pistol in one of the up-per rooms, and attempted to stab one of the servants with a Bowie knife. The Bowie had been popular with university students ever since the fall of the Alamo in 1836. Hall also broke Mrs. Gray's table furniture, earn-ing a dismissal by the board. In May 1842, Francis Patterson of North Carolina got drunk on a Saturday night and fired pistols several times on the Lawn. He then went to the Western Range and again opened fire with his pistols. He told the faculty he had drunk wine and cor-dials. He too was dismissed. The potential for injury, and even death, was so constant that when an expert in boxing and the broadsword ar-rived in January 1841 and proposed teaching the skills to students, chair-man Harrison didn't bother to pass the proposal along to the Board of Visitors.

Wicked women continued to sneak around the Lawn and into the dorms. In May 1842, Francis H. Jordan was called before the faculty on charges he had "entertained for several days in his room a woman of notoriously bad character." Jordan, of Luray, Virginia, denied the allegation, but "the Proctor had evidence that left not the smallest doubt as to the truth of the charge," according to the school's records. The proctor told the faculty "he had heard of Jordan's habits for some time and in passing his room one day heard him address language of this kind to some woman in his room. 'have I not always treated you as a lover.'" Jordan again denied the charges. He said he "admitted no woman of ill fame into his room at any time . . . a woman came to his room Wednesday morning whilst he was in bed. . . . He forbid her coming there, but she remained from sunrise till breakfast." Jordan said he told her to leave whenever he found her there. "She probably came to his room to seek shelter as she had been in jail and believed that she was pursued," according to school records. "There is another room on that block which she is in the habit of visiting. It cannot be expected of him to name the room. He knows that she has been introduced several times into other rooms."[3]

The commonplace antics and bad behavior had in the past brought on stricter rules and watchfulness. Proctors had scolded students, faculty had scolded proctors, and the Board of Visitors, in turn, had scolded professors. Nothing had worked. Tucker's arrival and leadership, however, led to a reawakening of Jefferson's belief that self-regulation, not rules, was all the discipline needed. Students could police themselves without the interrogation and oversight of others.

The first step came with a plea from the professors. On July 5, 1842, the faculty, with Harrison acting as chairman, asked the Board of Visitors to "repeal so much of the laws of the University as relates to the Uniform and further so to modify the law as to early rising as only to require the student to be ready for breakfast."[4] In short, professors were asking the board to scrap the detested Uniform Law, the source of so much student discontent and disobedience. The Early Rising Law—which required a student to be up in the predawn darkness—was equally hated, and now professors were saying it didn't matter what time students got up, as long as they made it to breakfast on time. Anger over the two rules had been the fuel for many of the riots and disturbances that had threatened the university's existence. The suggestion to remove the laws came from Tucker.

Even school officials had been ambiguous about the Uniform Law. One proctor, Arthur Brockenbrough, noted two years after the Uniform Law was passed in 1826 that "the objection to it is so great, I consider it rather as a prevention rather than an inducement to Students to come here."[5] The Early Rising Law had become a huge headache for officials tasked with enforcing it. The school's records are replete with names of lie-abed students. The request, reflecting a shift in the professors' attitudes, would represent a sea change in how the university was run. Doing away with these two onerous rules would bring the university closer to Jefferson's early vision. The faculty met that July 5 and adopted their recommendations, which were sent to the Board of Visitors meeting nearby. The board, which now included Jefferson's grandson Thomas Jefferson Randolph, pondered the ramifications of such a dramatic change. Would the elimination of the Uniform Law—which helped hide the students' wealth from the public—do more harm than good? Would the abolition of the Early Rising Law lead students to further indulge their sloth?

These are the questions the board debated. Several members were among those who had enacted the laws fifteen years earlier. Board member John H. Cocke, for instance, had stated that the Uniform Law was so critically important for holding down students' expenses that it must be enforced at all costs. Now he was one of those being asked to nullify the law. In the end, the board's fear of eliminating the rules tempered its decision. The board members acquiesced to the professors' request to eliminate the Early Rising Law but merely suspended the Uniform Law for one year. School rules limiting student expenditures, coupled with the 1838 state law forbidding merchants from giving students credit, would prevent students from wasting their fathers' money on fancy clothes, they hoped. They would watch over the following year to see if they had made the right choice.

Even before the loathsome rules were modified, the faculty, under Tucker, had begun to find a way to use the students' sense of honor to corral their behavior. The impetus, as usual, was another student brawl at a Charlottesville tavern. In December 1841, seven or eight students were drinking at Terrell's tavern and were "very noisey and some of them used abusive and obscene language."[6] Constable Summerson accosted the students and attempted to break up the rowdy group. But the lawman quickly found himself surrounded by a mob of some seventy to one hundred students who had rushed to the excitement. The records show that a "great deal of noise and disorder ensued with some damage to private property—some doors were broken by throwing of stones." The faculty believed C. C. May of Staunton and R. D. Gayle of Alabama were the ringleaders. May and Gayle were found in an ox-cart they had "taken from a negro." May said he had gone to the tavern to see Terrell's sister and Terrell had "took up a chair to knock him out." Gayle, meanwhile, said he had gone to the tavern to "see a bear" and somehow ended up in a fight with working stiffs in the town. He admitted to drinking spirits and "[did]n't remember anything after that." Both apologized.[7]

Previously, such a drunken free-for-all would have led to their dismissal. But now, the faculty, wiser after years of confrontations with students, tried a dramatic new tactic. The faculty persuaded the students to admit their guilt and compelled them to pledge on their honor not to repeat the offense. And, most important, the professors required each guilty student to get three classmates to pledge on their honor to report any of his misbehavior. This meant that the honor that students had invoked to hide offenses could now be used to bring them to light. It was an appeal that students could understand. "Now, it was an honorable, not dishonorable, act—at least in theory—to report on the misbehavior of students for whom sureties had pledged their word," noted Charles Coleman Wall Jr., the student who chronicled the school's early years in his dissertation.[8] The system seemed to work. One of the students from the December 15 ruckus violated his pledge and was swiftly dismissed without protest from his fellow students.

Even before the adoption of this new strategy, the professors had made a fledgling attempt to use honor as a means to prevent cheating on exams and improve the school's reputation for scholarship. Cheating had long been a problem, and in 1832, the school had suffered its first cheating scandal. In the midterm exam that year, "so many students, placed in the highest grade by the excellence of their papers, were found to have won that position by 'unfair means,' that every one who had been raised to it was compelled by the Faculty to prove his success was not to be attributed to improper assistance," according to the historian Bruce.[9] One student was expelled for cheating on the final exam that year. Three others had their diplomas rescinded. Cheating, however, continued.

In March 1841, the faculty passed a resolution that "no students shall bring into the lecture room at the hour appointed for the intermediate and final examination, to any of the schools, a portfolio, blank or printed books or make use of any other means of concealing notes in evasion of the laws which prescribe the mode of examination."[10]

In May 1841, the faculty passed a resolution stating that cheating at exams hurt the students and school alike. It is a "flagrant wrong to those who seek for honor by fair and honorable means, by reducing the value of the distinction which they obtain. Resolved, that the Faculty will refuse to confer a degree, or to allow distinction in every case in which they shall be satisfied, that the student has, at any examination for such degree or distinction, attempted to commit a fraud upon the Committee in any way or to any extent whatever."[11] The resolution targeted students who gave information as well as those who received it. The school would soon use the students' sacrosanct sense of honor to support those resolutions.

The university's new approach to taming student misbehavior was aided by a national temperance movement that swept the Lawn. Temperance leaders had been agitating against liquor since the 1820s, but only in 1842 did the movement take root at the university. Many students embraced the teetotaling lifestyle—to the probable dismay of the local tavern keepers. "We have just had a large meeting of the students to form a Temperance Society, and quite a respectable number have taken the teetotal pledge for the college course," wrote a delighted Professor Rogers to his brother Henry. "This I deem the happiest movement for the University that has ever been made, and I make no doubt that a large proportion of the students, if not all, will eventually join."[12] Rogers's optimism was wild-eyed, but for a time students corked their liquor bottles, adding a measure of stability at a critical moment in the university's life.

In October 1842, Tucker explained the new approach to discipline to assembled students. "I have always believed the most judicious and powerful means of governing youth was to appeal to their elevated feelings, to their pride, to their honor; to their native sense of propriety and right," Tucker said. He warned the students that disorder threatened the very existence of the university. "Is it indeed true that Virginia can maintain no Seminary because of the unruly character of her sons?"[13] Tucker admonished the students to attend class, to study, and to obey the rules—which now did not include the wearing of a school uniform or the need to be up by dawn. He promised, in turn, that students would be dealt with fairly under rules that were not arbitrary. Students, responding favorably to Tucker's explanation of the university's rules, asked him to put his speech in writing.

On the same day that professors asked the Board of Visitors to eliminate the Uniform Law and the Early Rising Law—July 4, 1842—they created an honor pledge. The pledge required students to affirm that they had not given or received any help on exams. At Tucker's suggestion, students would have to attach a certificate to their exams asserting on their honor that they had not cheated. Students complied willingly. Once again the professors had found a way to exploit the students' sense of honor to aid rather than hinder the university's operation. The honor pledge would evolve into the university's famed Honor System, which is still in effect today. Under the system, students accused by fellow students or professors of lying, cheating, or stealing face judgment by a student court. The only penalty for the guilty is expulsion.

The university appeared to be poised to make a fresh start. But looming ahead were several years of violence, one more major riot, and, finally, a public reckoning.

"Critical and Perilous Situation"

> I am so sure of the future approbation of posterity, and of the inestimable effect we shall have produced in the elevation of our country by what we have done, as that I cannot repent of the part I have borne in co-operation with my colleagues.
> —Jefferson to Cabell, Feb. 7, 1826

Student promises to stay sober and out of trouble once again proved empty. The year 1843 opened with a brawl between roughneck townies and students at a cheap, popular whorehouse located on the road between the university and the town. Students Addison White of Abingdon, Virginia, and John Wooten of North Carolina claimed they were defending themselves against ruffians who were trying to oust them from the bordello. The two were also accused of giving a "free negro a most cruel and unmerciful flogging." They both denied having anything to do with beating the free black man. White said he heard the man's "shrieks and went up and begged the person whipping him to desist."[1]

Other students were scolded for drinking, playing cards, resisting authority, and general carousing. While they pursued their pleasures with limitless energy, they were lazy students. Page after page of university records lists the names of students who failed to attend classes, made halfhearted attempts to complete assignments, or didn't bother to complete them at all. The long list of indolent scholars was a veritable blue book of the gentry. Many students had not come to Jefferson's university for an education but to polish their aristocratic credentials.

Their rank as gentlemen did not stop them from scuffling on the floor. In May, student Felix Gorman of Mississippi pulled his pistols on Samuel Oldham of Tennessee. Oldham, his sense of honor somehow offended by Gorman, had posted a threatening note on the Rotunda door. Gorman, expecting Oldham to make good on his threats, fetched his pistols from a lady friend who kept them for him. (Gorman would check in with her every few weeks to make sure his pistols were not rusting.) Securing the pistols had been a wise decision; two hours later Oldham arrived in Gorman's room, backed up by a gang of friends. All of them were armed with clubs. Oldham demanded "satisfaction," prompting Gorman to seize his own club, rush at Oldham, and knock him down with one swing. Oldham's friends rushed Gorman with their own clubs. Gorman then pulled his pistols and threatened "to shoot anyone who might assault him."[2]

Gorman was dismissed, but students were undeterred by punishment. That same month, student S. Dexter Otey of Lynchburg, Virginia, stabbed student Joseph B. Clements of Charlottesville during a scuffle. Otey was expelled.

The next year was no better. Students attacked houses in Charlottesville, broke windows, and staggered up and down the road, some in a state of "helpless intoxication."[3]

In October 1844, several students committed a "violent outrage" by attacking a house on the road between school and town. Students hurled stones into the house, "breaking the window glass, sash and blinds, and endangering lives of the occupants." The prime suspect, student James Galt Jr. of Fluvanna County, when confronted merely replied, "Well if I broke the window I can pay for it." He escaped with a reprimand.[4]

The end of 1844 brought the hammer blow that university officials had always feared. On December 22, the state House of Delegates, which had patiently stood by year after year as students ran amok at the University of Virginia, directed a committee to investigate "the past history and present condition of the school." Specifically, the Committee on Schools and Colleges was told to find out once and for all if the General Assembly should continue to give the university its annual $15,000.[5] The news struck the academic community like a bolt of lightning.

"My neighbors think and talk of nothing but the possible results of legislation upon our endowment," wrote Professor Rogers, now faculty chairman, to his brother Henry. Rogers professed confidence that the university would emerge from the threat of the investigation—and from the threat of the loss of state money—but his brother sensed that Rogers was "not at ease" about the matter.[6]

Indeed, Rogers had reason to be uneasy: the committee's investigation held devastating possibilities. The student body continued to number fewer than two hundred, which meant that income from student fees and room and board were low. The school still had debts totaling more than $17,000 and annual expenses of more than $21,000. Repair costs were also beginning to mount. Jefferson's buildings were now two decades old, and the wear and tear was becoming too pervasive to ignore. The school was now spending nearly $3,000 a year to shore up stone walls, whitewash buildings, repair columns and roofs, and clean out pumps. There were carpenters to hire, as well as blacksmiths, painters, locksmiths, and bricklayers. The university needed the state's $15,000 desperately.

Cabell and the Board of Visitors, along with Rogers and the other eight professors, viewed the legislature's action not only as a possibly fatal attack but as further proof of Virginia's cheapskate attitude toward its public university. They pointed out that the universities in Louisiana and Alabama were getting the same amounts or more from their state treasuries, yet they had nowhere near the reputation for scholarship as the University of Virginia. Officials argued that Jefferson's school offered the same quality education as Harvard, but Harvard did so with an annual income of $60,000, four times what Jefferson's school was receiving. Surely state legislators realized they were getting a big bang for their buck.

Friends of the university chimed in with their ideas on how to improve public perception of the school. One Staunton resident, William R. Johnson, suggested in a letter to Rogers that the University of Virginia should take control of the Virginia Military Institute. The Lexington institute, just five years old, was already popular and known statewide for the discipline of its cadets and its sense of frugality. Its reputation, in short, was the exact opposite of the university's. If the university gobbled up the institute, Johnson wrote, the university would enjoy some of the newer school's popularity:

> This seems to me desirable when I consider some of the sources of the prejudices against the University, her real or apparent want of discipline and economy, or when I look only at the frequent abuse which has been of late unjustly heaped upon her, and the strong feeling of hostility manifested in the present Legislature. . . . Some change in the organization of the University, if not its total destruction, seems to be meditated by its enemies, on the ground or the pretext of its expense and disorder; the military system seems to be the favorite of the day.[7]

To this letter Rogers responded that he and the other professors unanimously felt the university's disciplinary woes could be solved by the establishment of a campus police force (which, incidentally, would require an increase in state funding, not a decrease or elimination). Rogers also suggested that the University of Virginia's unruly students were probably no worse than students at other leading institutions, and the professors were "still strongly hopeful of steady and increased success, notwithstanding the ungenerous enmity of those who, from prejudice or ignorance, are laboring for our overthrow."[8]

Though Rogers's response to Johnson was polite and short, the House of Delegates committee demanded more detailed answers. Legislators wanted to know why they should continue to pay for a school widely perceived as a place where rich boys went to drink and raise hell and terrorize the peaceful community of Charlottesville. To Rogers, as faculty chairman, fell the task of responding.

In a fourteen-page report, Rogers defended the school by completely ignoring its disciplinary problems. Instead, he focused on its attainments. While the university had not yet lived up to its promise, Rogers conceded, it had dramatically improved the state's scientific and literary training. And it had done so using unique methods, he noted: its system of elective courses was still unusual in American higher education, and its use of classroom lectures to accompany textbooks was still a further peculiarity. The university, said the chairman, was proving every day that the two educational innovations were superior to the way all other American universities and colleges ran. Rogers, in short, was reminding legislators that the university was a bold experiment in education, conceived by Jefferson, but funded by a farsighted legislature.

Next, Rogers defended the school against allegations that professors were paid too extravagantly. The school's professors, he noted, averaged an annual salary of $2,350 in 1844, a sum in line with the pay of professors at Princeton, West Point, and the Universities of Pennsylvania and South Carolina. Considering the amount of teaching that went on at the University of Virginia, Rogers concluded, the state's annual outlay of $15,000 "cannot fail to be regarded as but a very moderate contribution."[9] The House of Delegates accepted Rogers's report.

But, as if on cue, students again rioted. The 1845 riots had no roots in any student grievances, such as the Uniform Law or the earlier faculty crackdown on the military company, but sprang from students' unfettered sense of mischief. The timing could not have been worse.

In late 1844, a group of students had banded together to form a "musical" band known as the Calathumpians. Their express purpose was to create mayhem across the Lawn, or, as one of the group's members said, to engage in "fun—and frolic and childish folly." Tooting horns, beating drums, and torturing other instruments, the group paraded up and down the precincts in the darkness, denying classmates and professors sleep.[10]

Weeks passed, and the group became rowdier. The Calathumpian band, which some of the better students had now left, according to early accounts, began to plot to bring the school year to an early close. In February 1845 they found a cause to set their plot in motion. That day, three students were suspended for disorderly conduct at one of the hotels. That night, the band members organized a protest parade. But instead of blowing horns and banging drums, they donned masks and attacked the hotel and the home of chairman Rogers with sticks and stones, breaking down a door and smashing windows. The faculty ordered the proctor, Willis Woodley, to get the names of the miscreants so they could be turned over to a grand jury.

The determination to go straight to the civil authorities calmed the precincts, but only briefly. The Calathumpians reassembled to hurl stones against the parlor window of a professor's pavilion while ladies were in the room. Then, on April 2, one member of the roving band startled the wife of the chemistry professor, Robert Rogers—chairman Rogers's brother, who had arrived in 1842—by rapping on the window. Professor Rogers was out at the time, but when he returned, he found his wife still shaken. When he heard the band returning, he quickly stepped outside his pavilion and hid behind a pillar. As one of the students stepped toward his front door, Rogers leapt out, picked up the student, and carried him inside. When the other students threatened to intervene, Rogers warned them that he was armed and would shoot. They left.

But the nightly disturbances only grew worse. On April 14 the students hurled stones and wood against the doors of the pavilions, smashed the blinds, and shattered the windows. The professors' wives and children were now in a state of terror. Two days later students— and possibly some students who had already been dismissed—rode up and down the arcades firing pistols. The Lawn became a racetrack, as one student and a former student raced horses—stolen from the proctor's stable—while other students wagered ice creams and money. The following three nights brought no respite. Students once again attacked the pavilions, hurling stones at windows where the glass had already been shattered. "It was said that, on the following morning, several of the houses had the aspect of having been bombarded by a mob," the historian Bruce noted.[11] The Rotunda did not escape the students' violence: two of its doors were battered open, and many of its windows lay in shards.

Professors appealed to the students, but in vain. They then looked to the better students to help calm the passions of their classmates, or possibly to identify them, but their pleas met with indifference: ringleaders of the riots had threatened to beat any student who worked to stop the mayhem. The professors imposed a lockdown—prohibiting students from leaving the precincts. On April 19, the faculty abruptly shut down the school, locking classrooms and suspending lectures. Professor Tucker, meanwhile, fearful for the safety of his two sons,

H. Tudor and St. George, pleaded for permission to send the boys to Richmond. His fellow professors refused.

On Sunday, April 20, two days after seeking the advice of the Board of Visitors executive committee, the professors decided they had suffered enough: they agreed to call in the civil magistrates and the county sheriff to put down the disorder. The move was a measure of last resort, partly because professors considered it an admission that they themselves couldn't stop the student misbehavior, and partly because the General Assembly would surely learn of the unrest once civil authorities got involved.

The students caught wind of the coming intervention, held a mass meeting, and swore to each other that no one would testify. Still, the following day local magistrates arrived on the precincts, and an armed guard was placed around the Rotunda. "We have so large an admixture this year of cowardly rowdies amongst us that some signal demonstration of the proper mode of dealing with them cannot help being salutary, and it will be useful for them to learn that we are prepared to punish their insults on the spot," chairman Rogers had written two weeks earlier. Now he and the other professors were ready to make good on the threat.[12]

The proctor summoned twenty students to appear before the magistrates. Many of the students, though, simply vanished. In the afternoon, seventy of them, alarmed at the possibility that the militia would be called in, gathered at the university to debate their course of action. They disbanded after pledging to end the disruptions. But they were too late. Albemarle County high sheriff Benjamin Ficklin marched a force of two hundred armed men onto the Lawn, turning the precincts into occupied territory.

As they had before in similar circumstances, the students claimed to be outraged. They gathered again that night to pass a resolution that expressed bafflement that the faculty would not accept their pledge to restore peace. Calling in the militia, the students said, was an affront to their honor. Abruptly, about 125 students withdrew from the university (initial enrollment in 1844 had been only 194). Cabell, realizing that the university was in a "critical & perilous situation,"[13] hastily summoned the Board of Visitors, and on April 23 it endorsed the faculty's response. The students were in revolt, the officials refused to back down, and the university was at a standstill.

Classes resumed on April 25, but word of the rioting had spread across Virginia. What, the public was now asking, was wrong at the University of Virginia? Why was it constantly in turmoil? Why should we continue to pay for it? "The animosity to the University which lurked chronically in many minds because of political or religious prejudices, seized upon the notorious course of events there as a weapon for blackening its prospects beyond recovering," Bruce noted, summing up the storm of negative publicity that washed over the school.[14]

For the rest of the year, the fate of the university hung in the balance. Supporters defended it, opponents thrashed it, legislators debated it, and the common people wondered how it would all turn out. Stoking the heated discussion were the newspapers. "Public rumour and the newspaper have already spread far and wide the reports of our riots," lamented chairman Rogers. He added: "The annals of college disturbances could hardly furnish another narrative as disgraceful to the character of the youth of the country as the history of this would be."[15]

A war of words erupted between the *Richmond Enquirer*, the bastion of Republican thinking, and the *Richmond Whig*, a steady opponent of the university since its inception. The debate over the university's future became a scrum between rival editors. On April 29, the day Rogers complained about the publicity, the *Whig* published a front-page account of the riots, which the writer described as "a sad and most disgraceful affair." "Most of the Students," the article stated, "have left; the Faculty, it is understood, will resign; and for the present the College appears to be broken up." The *Whig* claimed five hundred militiamen were now in charge of the university.[16] The *Whig* followed up the incendiary article on May 2, when it published a student's account of the "disturbances."[17]

The *Enquirer* responded on May 6 by publishing the faculty's version of events, penned by Rogers. In his letter, Rogers contended that calling out the militia was the only way to stop the riots, and he noted that the Board of Visitors in its April 23 meeting had resolved to take the same steps if there were future riots. The *Enquirer* prefaced the article with its own commentary that essentially ignored the riots as yesterday's news: "We see nothing in the recent unfortunate disorders to prove a radical and permanent injury to the College, and we invoke all its friends, whether parents or students, to suffer not their ardor to be dampened, but to rally with new energy to the support of an Institution that has shed the light of education over Virginia, and has given proofs of its important benefits in many of her distinguished sons; now in the State and National Councils."[18]

But critics were not to be dissuaded by the *Enquirer*'s gilded words. Three days later the *Whig* published a piece in which it said the students were no doubt "in the wrong" but nevertheless criticized the professors for overreacting. The proper response, the *Whig*'s editor opined, would have been to ignore the weeks and months of nightly disturbances until the students grew tired and gave up.[19] The newspaper kept up the criticism on May 16, arguing that the professors' use of military force "could only be the act of Philosophers, unskilled in the ways of the world, and ignorant of the arts by which to govern men."[20]

The *Charlottesville Jeffersonian*, a newspaper whose allegiances were never in doubt, accused the *Whig* of "vandalism," describing its attacks on the university and the professors as a deliberate attempt to pull the school apart brick by brick:

> The Richmond Whig seems determined to destroy the University if it can either by withholding the annual appropriation of $15,000, which the state gives this institution, or by building up another College or University in Richmond, or by both.
>
> Far better would it be for the State to appropriate $20,000 a year, and then the fees to the professors might be abolished, and the indigent and needy youth educate themselves at a very trifling expense;—and in this way a host of teachers might spring up in all parts of the State; and instead of 200 students 600 would begin attendance on the Lectures.[21]

At this point the *Enquirer* weighed in with more opinions. A May 30 article signed by "A Friend to the University" blamed the low attendance on the high cost of enrollment, which the writer in turn blamed on the exorbitant salaries of the professors. On June 3, an *Enquirer* piece laid the blame at the feet of the legislature: had the General Assembly only adopted Jefferson's plan years ago to fund public schools, more young boys would eventually have found their way to the University of Virginia. The *Morgantown Mountaineer*, meanwhile, speaking on behalf of the state's western residents, simply dismissed the university's value altogether, calling its reckless students "emphatically the worthless sons of rich Eastern Virginia aristocrats, who rejoice in the prostration of Western Virginia."[22]

In June, the *Richmond Whig and Public Advertiser* began in earnest a campaign to create a university in Richmond, a move that would, in effect, kill Jefferson's school, since the legislature could only afford to support one. To create enthusiasm for its plan, the newspaper boasted that a university in Richmond would only cost half as much to operate, assured Richmond parents that their sons would remain under their watchful eyes, and urged landowners to donate land for the school. "But our emphatic appeal is to the poor men of Richmond: Which among us does not desire to educate his son thoroughly?" the newspaper asked before launching into an attack on Jefferson's school. "The University —erected by the People at an expense of hundreds of thousands, and sustained since its commencement at the cost of additional hundreds of thousands—the University is inaccessible to us: Other Institutions are scarcely less beyond our reach. With a University at our door, we could completely educate our sons at a cost within the limits of our means."[23]

The paper followed up with an article that suggested "too much money has been wasted upon" the University of Virginia. The writer closed by arguing that the state's annual payment to the university should be reduced.[24]

Other newspapers across the state joined in the debate, and many of them urged the university's friends and alumni to be more energetic in its defense. Cabell and the other Visitors asked Tucker, respected statewide for the sharpness of his legal mind, to draft a petition to the General Assembly to set up a court near the university. Tucker's health was waning, though, and the Visitors didn't pursue the idea. The Visitors also asked Cabell to persuade the legislature to forbid dismissed students from staying within five miles of the university, but that plan likewise went nowhere. The board even toyed with the idea of establishing a president over the university—a move that would have pained Jefferson—but the idea evaporated along with the other schemes.

However, the board did make several clever moves to shore up the school's tenuous position. Aware that many Virginians still viewed it as a haven for the dissolute rich, the board proposed a plan in which one poor student from every senatorial district in the state would receive a free university education—as long as the General Assembly paid for his board. If the General Assembly was truly concerned about the state's poor, it now had an opportunity to remedy the problem.

The board also proposed the creation of a history and English department. The move was purely offensive. At a time when state legislators were contemplating a cut in funding, Cabell moved to squeeze them for more.

In a final and far-reaching move, the board made two critical new hires. Both George Tucker and Henry St. George Tucker, who between them had seen years of student recklessness, had submitted their resignations. Now, the board quickly filled their slots with two men known as pillars of moral rectitude, men whose religion and reputations were widely esteemed.

John B. Minor was tapped to become law professor, a position he would hold for fifty years, earning him the distinction of signing more law diplomas than anyone in the country's history. Born in 1813 in Louisa County, Virginia, Minor began life with a reputation as a weakling. To improve his health, he began walking. At one point he walked through the states of Ohio and New York. His regimen worked: his stamina became legendary. He entered the University of Virginia as a student in 1831 and stayed for three years. He later married Professor Davis's daughter. An Episcopalian, he considered his religion the "master-chord in his life."[25] He taught Sunday school to slaves and a Bible class to students. One of the university's prominent academic buildings bears his name today.

To fill the moral philosophy post vacated by George Tucker, the board chose William Holmes McGuffey, a balding, bespectacled scholar of philosophy already known for putting together the phenomenally successful series of textbooks known today as the McGuffey Readers. Born in 1800 in Pennsylvania, McGuffey was ordained a Presbyterian minister in 1829. A teetotaler, he believed in temperance and the moral righteousness of Christianity, and he loved to teach children. With the hiring of McGuffey and Minor, the board had instantly crafted a more pious public image for the school, just when it needed it most.

The board was not alone in the effort to save the university. The school's alumni came to its defense as well. Meeting in the Rotunda on July 3 and 4, the former students chose seven of the society's most prominent members to carry out a carefully orchestrated public relations campaign with Cabell. Cabell, as rector, would present the university's case before the General Assembly. Meanwhile, the seven alumni would draft their own statement on behalf of the school.

The seven alumni—all Virginians—were an argument themselves for the worth of the university; their lives and careers were proof of its benefit to the state. History records them as Franklin Minor, a state legislator from Albemarle; Willis Bocock, a state legislator from Buckingham; Jefferson's grandson George Wythe Randolph, a navy man who would later become the Confederacy's secretary of war; William Frazier, a state legislator from Augusta County; Egbert Watson, an Albemarle judge; John B. Young, a prosecutor from Henrico County; and William C. Carrington, a Charlottesville lawyer. These men did not just have friends in high places—they lived and moved in high places themselves.

The document they drafted argued forcefully for the continued financial support of the university, while attacking head-on the common criticisms against the school: its godlessness, the extravagance of its student expenses, professor salaries, and the scandalous behavior of its students. The committee of seven also appealed to their fellow Virginians' sense of posterity: "Let not the well matured work of JEFFERSON, and MADISON, and MONROE, and CABELL, and JOHNSON, be pulled to pieces in a moment, at the thoughtless bidding of irresponsible anonymous writers and reckless reformers."[26] In a state proud of its rich history, these were powerful words.

But the alumni's main line of attack was to argue that the school was no more expensive than any other school in the nation and the money it received from Virginia paled in comparison to state funding of other schools such as Harvard. The university cost the state $15,000 annually, amounting to only 1.25 cents per Virginia resident. The availability of the university meant Virginia's sons could stay in the state to obtain an education. The alumni calculated that 2,338 students had attended lectures at the university since its opening and had spent $422,800—money that would have in theory gone outside the state if the university had never been built.

Factoring in money that out-of-state students brought to the school, the alumni estimated that the university had generated $1.3 million for the state—double the sum spent on the school and nearly $30 million in today's money.

"What other great work in which Virginia has invested her funds, has yielded her a richer harvest of fruits? and this without estimating the important benefits of education and science it has disseminated throughout our limits, and which have blessed all classes of citizens, rich and poor, high and low, in giving us more skilful and better informed positions, lawyers, farmers, schoolmasters, divines, judges and law-makers," the alumni wrote.[27]

As for the chronic complaint that only the rich could afford to attend the university, the alumni argued that an average student would need only $332 for one school year. The alumni said the sum was trifling and considered "the clamor in the country in regard to the great expense necessary to students at the university to be groundless. . . . If young men spend more than this, parents and guardians must blame them, and not lay the extravagance of their sons and wards at the door of the university. . . . Young men will wear clothes and spend pocket money to suit their tastes and conditions in life, at whatever school, college or university they may be sent to or indeed even at home."[28]

Were professors paid too much? To that constant question, the alumni responded that an average professor earned less than $2,400—not even as much as South Carolina paid its professors. In addition, professors at other colleges were assisted by tutors who lightened their workload.

The churches' distrust of Jefferson's religious views had continued. Now the alumni moved to counter that animosity by contending that the perceptions of the university as a godless institution were "wholly unfounded."[29] The alumni noted that a chapel had been built next to the Rotunda within the last several years. Furthermore, the university invited chaplains of all the denominations to preach in the precincts on a rotating basis. The students, professors, and staff chipped in $500 to $800 a year to pay the chaplains' salaries. Students and professors also paid for Sunday school and the support of a Bible society. Though Jefferson gave religion no formal place in the university, it flourished nonetheless. "To all outward appearance, religion is as much respected and as liberally supported at the university as elsewhere, and this without the disadvantage of even the semblance of sectarian influence."[30]

After tackling religion, the alumni addressed the issue that had roiled the state for the past three months and sharpened the threat to the university's existence—the April riots. The alumni boldly asserted that the riots weren't so bad and happened all the time at other colleges and were part of the inexplicable fabric of college life. In addition, the alumni charged that the General Assembly and the people of Virginia were overreacting; riots at schools in other states never threatened their existence: "It is owing simply to the fact, that the communities in which they are situated, the whole body of the people, instead of pouncing upon the college, and threatening to tear it down, (as if disappointed that the rioters had left their work unfinished) had uniformly extended to the authorities a generous confidence; have come forward to aid and not to embarrass them; and instead of giving a willing ear to the complaints of the rioters, and the disaffected, have leaned to the side of law, order and authority, against insubordination and rebellion."[31]

Why, then, should the University of Virginia's future be at stake? "When will Virginians learn to cherish their own institutions, to extend a like generous confidence to their constituted authorities, and to come up to their aid and support in all their difficulties?"[32]

The alumni had made their argument. Cabell would now make his own pitch to save the university he had cofounded with Jefferson. In his annual report to the General Assembly, Cabell carefully echoed the alumni's talking points and at times blamed the legislature for its lack of support. Cabell said the riots were not proof of any "inherent defect" in the university but were largely caused by students who had been dismissed.[33] The General Assembly, he suggested, should have granted the university the power to keep dismissed students at a distance from the school. He said the university's graduates had become teachers and ministers throughout the state; the university was cheap compared to the cost of Harvard, Yale, and William and Mary; and it had become the state's premier school of higher education. Cabell also pleaded for continued state support; unlike other, religious-affiliated colleges, such as Harvard and William and Mary, the University of Virginia could not rely on the private donations of religious benefactors. State support was critical.

In January 1846, the General Assembly—where the Whig party had lost power to the Democrats the year before—sent a team of legislators to investigate the school and get a firsthand look at what exactly was going on. The visit followed more months of student unrest. Though professors and townspeople had long grown tired of student misbehavior, the students burned a tar barrel on the Lawn and resumed their nightly parades with horns and bells. That month the investigating committee sent the faculty a letter requesting their testimony on the affairs of the university. Professor Edward Courtenay, now the chairman of the faculty, rushed off to see Cabell. After conferring with the rector and other board members, he wrote a note to the investigators saying faculty members would be happy to testify in writing or in person. Courtenay personally met with the investigators to assure them of the faculty's full cooperation.

Students, however, were much less cooperative. To the horror of school officials, the students appeared eager to draw the investigators' attention to their disregard for authority. They stole a second tar barrel from the basement of the proctor's office and set it ablaze on the Lawn—scorching a hideous black streak into the spacious expanse. Acrid black smoke billowed into the air throughout the night as students set off firecrackers, fired their pistols, and "made other discordant noise." As the board members housed within the precincts tried to sleep, students lit up another tar barrel at midnight. Students with blackened faces and wearing "blanket caps" created a "scene of great riot and noise."[34]

The next morning, Cabell, Courtenay, and Professor Harrison traveled to Charlottesville to testify before the investigators about the April riots. That night, students resumed their noisy antics on the Lawn. Then, as if to send a loud and defiant message to the General Assembly, students marched off to the house where the investigators were staying. The following day, January 23, the investigators wrapped up their hearings with testimony from members of the Board of Visitors and a statement from Courtenay.

In the end, despite the students' antics, the General Assembly was swayed by the answers they received from visitors and professors, by the testimony of the university's distinguished alumni, and by the machinations of Cabell. The investigators concluded that funding should continue. The university was an ornament to the state and, despite years of turmoil, was serving a noble purpose, the committee said in its report. The school's terrible reputation, established in its early years under Jefferson's lax disciplinary system, was no longer deserved—despite the latest riot. The university had improved, but the public's perception had not, the General Assembly stated. "During this experimental stage of its career, it is well known that habits of dissipation and extravagance, with other offensive irregularities, prevailed among the students to a lamentable extent," according to the report. "The unfavourable impression thus occasioned in the public mind, far outlasting any reasonable cause in the government of the university, has continued, though with greatly diminished force to obstruct its advancement even to the present day." The report conveniently ignored years of violence, riots, and the murder of a professor.[35]

Still, the critics had been defeated. The allies of the university had won. The war was over. The university had survived several riots, years of student stupidity and violence, the enmity of the religious establishment, the animosity of Jefferson's political opponents, disease, bad publicity, and the vacillating governance of its own Board of Visitors.

Jefferson had created an institution too unique to destroy. Cabell, the ultimate Jefferson disciple, had spent his health and life to keep it alive. "We have had a most interesting session," Cabell wrote his wife after the investigating committee left Charlottesville. "Had I not assembled the Board of Visitors, the days of the University would probably have been numbered. At one time I was greatly alarmed. But I am much relieved, as the Committee seemed to be most favorable impressed by the examinations which they made."[36]

Indeed they were.

A New Kind of University

Jefferson, twenty years after his death, had finally triumphed. His vision, the dream of his old age, had won out after a perilous birth and infancy. As a result of his efforts to create the university, Jefferson's already controversial reputation had suffered a blow. Enemies had lashed out at him personally, but to the end, he remained optimistic that history would vindicate him. "The attempt [to create the university] ran foul of so many local interests, of so many personal views, and of so much ignorance, and I have been considered as so particularly its promoter, that I see evidently a great change of sentiment towards myself," Jefferson had lamented to his friend Cabell as early as January 1825, just months before the school's opening. "I have ever found in my progress through life, that, acting for the public, if we do always what is right, the approbation denied in the beginning will surely follow us in the end."[1]

Though the path was longer than Jefferson envisioned, his school ultimately became a preeminent institution. His idea of intellectual investigations unhampered by theology would not only prevail at his university but would spread throughout the nation. His university endured the criticism of those who resisted change; later universities would more easily abandon the old ways and experiment with the new.

In a short twenty years, Jefferson and his disciples had turned a scraggly field on the outskirts of a little river town into a unique institution. Where pigs and cows once roamed over raw red clay, now the model of a secular public American university rooted itself into the landscape and flourished.

School officials had begged for more money from the state since Jefferson conceived the idea of the university; with renewed confidence, the General Assembly finally upped its annual contribution to $40,000, a stunning windfall.

Students throughout the southern states began to trek from their small hamlets and large plantations to Charlottesville. In the school's first fifty years, roughly 5,400 Virginians attended the school. North Carolina contributed 880 students; South Carolina, 520; Florida, 67; Georgia, 820; Alabama, 575; Mississippi, 365; Louisiana, 265; Texas, 135; Arkansas, 48; Tennessee, 230; Kentucky, 203; Missouri, 110; and Maryland and the District of Columbia, 390. Only 155 students came from northern states. Importantly, enrollment at the University of Virginia equaled and exceeded enrollment at rivals Harvard and Yale by the 1850s. Jefferson's plan had worked.

The school soon expanded from its original eight departments to nineteen, including engineering, agriculture, and astronomy, bringing the curriculum more in line with Jefferson's early vision. Private supporters stepped forward with money. Donations began to pour in. By 1885, the university had received the whopping sum of nearly $900,000.

Meanwhile, the school began turning out southern leaders. In its first fifty years, it produced 6 governors, 7 lieutenant governors, 62 congressmen (and 31 Confederate congressmen), 2 cabinet ministers, 167 judges, 348 members of state legislatures, 59 authors and artists, 22 mayors, and 8 state attorneys general. And the university managed all this despite the catastrophic effects of the Civil War. University students and alumni rallied to the Confederate battle flag. A large number of Confederate engineers were university graduates, as were most of the ranking staff officers. Two of the Confederacy's secretaries of war were University of Virginia men—George Wythe Randolph and James A. Seddon. More than three hundred alumni were killed in battle.

Throughout the southern states in the nineteenth century, the University of Virginia was known simply as "The University," a sobriquet that captures the esteem and adoration of a region steeped in ignorance and violence.

Despite that success, the university that evolved was not quite what Jefferson planned. Eventually, the Board of Visitors would name the school's first president—Edwin Alderman—in 1904. The office of president struck Jefferson as undemocratic. Perhaps equally troubling to him was the fact that in his day college presidents were always leading churchmen. So opposed was Jefferson to the concept of a president that when the Board of Visitors created the position and offered it to the attorney general of the United States in 1826, Jefferson wrote a strong protest in the school's records. When the attorney general declined the position—possibly because of the great statesman's vehement opposition—the board would not attempt to create the position again until Alderman's appointment.

Also changed was Jefferson's plan to allow students to spend as little as one year at the school studying courses that could prove practical to them. The university eventually became a four-year school that granted degrees.

But Jefferson's big ideas prevailed. "It is surprising to observe how Jefferson anticipated many of the modern educational ideas which have come into conspicuous favor since his day," wrote N. H. R. Dawson, a U.S. commissioner of education, in 1887.[2]

More recently, the historians John Brubacher and Willis Rudy described Jefferson as "the first great protagonist of the public secular university."[3] According to Brubacher and Rudy,

> The university which Thomas Jefferson established at Charlottesville in Virginia was America's first real state university. It is an authentic example of this type for a number of reasons. First of all, it aimed from the beginning to give more advanced instruction than the existing colleges, to permit students to specialize and to enjoy the privileges of election. Its course of study when it opened for instruction in 1825 was much broader than that which was customary at the time. Secondly, the University of Virginia was by the express intent of its constitution a thoroughly public enterprise, rather than a private or quasi-public one. Finally, its early orientation was distinctly and purposefully secular and non-denominational. In all of this, it represented the most thoroughgoing embodiment of the "revolutionary" spirit of the Enlightenment to be found in American higher education during the first decades of the 19th century.[4]

As Jefferson himself once wrote of his university, "It belongs not to political parties and religious sects as a field in which they may carry on their conflicts for predominance. It belongs simply to the people, and to all the people whether they belong to political parties or to none; whether they belong to religious sects or have no religious connections."[5]

Following Jefferson's lead, the nation's other public universities eventually became secular, uncontrolled by church denominations. (So advanced was Jefferson's thinking, though, that his secular university would still be novel into the early twentieth century, when some public universities still forced students to attend chapel.) In Jefferson's time, universities were merely another avenue by which religion exercised its influence on society. Each denomination founded its own schools. When states founded schools, they only did so with the blessings of the church. However, the revolution that Jefferson had set in motion would not be turned back.

Jefferson's curriculum was a marvel of practicality. Under the old system, developed by the church, students learned Greek, Latin, and mathematics to prepare them for the professions of law, medicine, and the clergy. So it had been for centuries. Jefferson's courses excluded theology, dramatically shifting one of the key roles of universities. He followed that innovation by introducing courses he felt had more practical value to students, especially to those who would only attend for one or two years. In Jefferson's school, students could learn modern languages, such as French, Spanish, Italian, and German. Students could study architecture, astronomy, geography, chemistry, mineralogy, botany, political economy, history, politics, and ethics—courses that could be found in any college catalog today. Jefferson also tinkered with teaching methods. Other American schools taught by rote memorization. Professors read to students from textbooks. Jefferson demanded that professors interact with their students, answering and asking questions. Professors truly lectured instead of merely reading out loud.

In another dramatic change, Jefferson devised and promoted an elective system within American higher education at a time when most students were required to take identical courses, no matter their interest or ambition in life. Jefferson crafted a system in which students could choose an area of interest to study. That unique elective scheme quickly spread, and by 1884 at least thirty-five southern colleges and universities were using it. After two hundred years of existence, even hidebound Harvard eventually reformed its curriculum along Jefferson's lines.

Finally, Jefferson's reliance on honor as the foundation of student discipline was realized, and it saved his university. Other schools, following the University of Virginia, eventually adopted their own codes of honor. Before the University of Virginia's Honor System was embraced, students were treated as children. Professors spied on them and imposed severe punishments for minor infractions. Jefferson's belief was that students would police themselves. The belief proved erroneous because the students who arrived on campus were not the mature young men he anticipated. Consequently, the students misbehaved, and the professors imposed rules, creating a police state in the precincts, which Jefferson had tried so hard to avoid. The formal adoption of the Honor System in 1842 would eventually transform students into overseers of their own behavior, which Jefferson had envisioned so many years previously. The Honor System, aided by the civilizing effects of temperance and religion, helped tame the students by recognizing them as men of honor and appealing to their own view of themselves as gentlemen.

The school's Honor System—which helped save the school in its infancy—is still in place. The only crimes under the code, born of so much violence and pain, are lying, cheating, and stealing. Expulsion remains the only choice of punishment if a student is found guilty. Though referendums to allow alternate, milder punishments are routinely held, they are routinely voted down by students, who run the Honor System themselves.

Over the course of nearly 170 years, dozens of students, judged by their classmates, have been expelled for violating the Honor System. Even today, students must sign a pledge vowing to follow the Honor System before they can become university students.

Students at the university today are still taught according to the Jeffersonian method. As Jefferson said, "The university will be based on the illimitable freedom of the human mind. For here we are not afraid to follow truth wherever it may lead, nor to tolerate error so long as freedom is left free to combat it."[6]

A Note on Sources

The authors relied on a wealth of primary source material, much of it found in the University of Virginia's Special Collections Library, to write *Rot, Riot, and Rebellion: Mr. Jefferson's Struggle to Save the University That Changed America*. Crucial to the undertaking, of course, were the letters of Thomas Jefferson, James Madison, James Monroe, Joseph Cabell, and Edgar Allan Poe. Also heavily relied upon were the handwritten notes of the university's faculty chairmen, the minutes of the faculty meetings, minutes from the university's Board of Visitors, and sundry letters from students, their parents, school administrators and professors, and travelers who happened to pass through Charlottesville during the university's early years. Several professors also left brief memoirs that proved indispensable. Newspapers of the time that provided material include the *Richmond Enquirer*, the *Richmond Whig*, and the *Jeffersonian Republican*. The diary of student Charles Ellis was especially helpful, as were the letters written by Jefferson's family members. The authors are also indebted to the few history books written nearly a century ago about the university: Philip Alexander Bruce's five-volume *University of Virginia*, John Patton's *Jefferson, Cabell, and the University of Virginia*, and Paul Barringer and James Garnett's *University of Virginia*. Several student dissertations provided background information, chief among them Charles Coleman Wall Jr.'s "Students and Student Life at the University of Virginia, 1825–1861."

Notes

Introduction

1. Powell, *Bring Out Your Dead*, xvii.
2. University of Virginia, "Journals of the Chairman of the Faculty, 1827–1864" (hereafter cited as "Journals of the Chairman"), Mar. 17, 1833.
3. "Journals of the Chairman," Mar. 24, 1833.
4. Jefferson et al., *Report of the Commissioners*, n.p.
5. Bruce, *History of the University*, 2:259.
6. Freeman, *Affairs of Honor*, xvi.
7. Ibid., xx.
8. Ibid., xvi.
9. Wyatt-Brown, *Shaping of Southern Culture*, 192.
10. Williams, *Dueling in the Old South*, 8.
11. Jefferson and Cabell, *Early History of the University*, 260.
12. Ibid., 289.
13. Wall, "Students and Student Life," 44.
14. Emerson, *Journals of Ralph Waldo Emerson*, 4:275.

1. "Acts of Great Extravagance"

1. Henry Stokes to Colin Stokes, Apr. 2, 1839, Alderman Library, University of Virginia.
2. "Journals of the Chairman," Mar. 19, 1839.
3. Ibid.
4. Ibid.
5. Ibid.

2. The Ugly Beginning

1. Parton, *Life of Thomas Jefferson*, 569.
2. Ibid., 210.
3. Merwin, *Thomas Jefferson*, 116.
4. Jefferson and Cabell, *Early History of the University*, 128.
5. Jefferson, *Notes*, 269.
6. Parton, *Life of Thomas Jefferson*, 216–217.
7. Patton, *Jefferson, Cabell, and the University*, 10.
8. Ibid., 15.
9. Shawen, "Casting of a Lengthened Shadow," 65.
10. Ibid., 68.
11. Ibid. At about the same time, Jefferson also failed to win support for another plan—to emancipate slaves and give some education to those who would one day be free. He informally proposed the scheme to a member of the General

Assembly, but legislators rejected it. Except as laborers and servants, blacks never figured into any of his designs for a university. Despite his revolutionary ideas about freedom and equality, Jefferson considered blacks mentally inferior humans and owned slaves until the day he died.

12. Adams, *Thomas Jefferson and the University*, 48.

3. Building a University in Virginia

1. Rosenfeld, *American Aurora*, 112.
2. Brodie, *Intimate History*, 321.
3. Larson, *Magnificent Catastrophe*, 70.
4. Ibid., 169.
5. Hamilton, *Papers*, 24:576.
6. Larson, *Magnificent Catastrophe*, 173.
7. Ibid., 172.
8. Parton, *Life of Thomas Jefferson*, 572.
9. Ibid., 573.
10. Ibid., 572.
11. Ibid.
12. Adams, *Thomas Jefferson and the University*, 61.
13. Tanner, "Joseph C. Cabell," 10.
14. Ibid., 13.
15. Ibid., 8.
16. Barringer and Garnett, *University of Virginia*, 318–319.
17. Jefferson and Cabell, *Early History of the University*, 40.
18. Shawen, "Casting of a Lengthened Shadow," 188.
19. "Report of the Central College Board of Visitors," Jan. 6, 1818.
20. "Minutes of the Board of Visitors of Central College," May 5, 1817.
21. "Interview with Edmund Bacon, ca. 1860." In *22 Documents Concerning the Founding of the University of Virginia*, Electronic Text Center, University of Virginia Library, http://etext.lib.virginia.edu/toc/modeng/public/Jef14Gr.html.
22. Jefferson and Cabell, *Early History of the University*, 88.
23. Tanner, "Joseph C. Cabell," 129.
24. Ibid.
25. Shawen, "Casting of a Lengthened Shadow," 261.
26. Madison, *Writings*, 126.
27. Shawen, "Casting of a Lengthened Shadow," 379.
28. Jefferson and Cabell, *Early History of the University*, 140.
29. Ibid., 142.
30. "Legislature of Virginia: Extracts from the Journal of the House of Delegates," *Richmond Enquirer*, Jan. 19, 1819.
31. Untitled newspaper article, *Richmond Enquirer*, Jan. 21, 1819.
32. Jefferson and Cabell, *Early History of the University*, 150.
33. Ibid., 218.
34. Coleman and Perrin, *Amazing Erie Canal*, 41.
35. Jefferson and Cabell, *Early History of the University*, 169.
36. John Rice, "An Excursion Into the Country," *Virginia Evangelical and Literary Magazine*, Dec. 1818, 547.
37. Toynbee, "English Culture in Virginia," 39.
38. Jefferson, *Writings*, 15:403–406.
39. Jefferson and Cabell, *Early History of the University*, 201.

4. "Vicious Irregularities"

1. Tutwiler, *Address*, 10.
2. Smith, *First Forty Years*, 223.
3. Ibid., 229.
4. "Minutes of the Faculty of the University of Virginia," Oct. 2, 1825.
5. Tutwiler, *Address*, 8.
6. Jefferson, *Public and Private Papers*, 154–155.
7. Martha Jefferson Randolph to Ellen W. Randolph Coolidge, Oct. 13, 1825, Ellen Wayles Randolph Coolidge Correspondence, University of Virginia, transcript in Family Letters Digital Archive, Thomas Jefferson Foundation, Inc., http://www.monticello.org/familyletters.
8. "Minutes of the Faculty," Oct. 4, 1825.
9. Jefferson, *Writings*, 18:343.
10. "Minutes of the Faculty," Oct. 5, 1825.
11. Ibid.
12. Ibid.
13. Jefferson, *Writings*, 18:344.
14. "Minutes of the Faculty," Oct. 5, 1825.
15. Cornelia J. Randolph to Ellen W. Randolph Coolidge, July 13, 1825, Ellen Wayles Randolph Coolidge Correspondence, University of Virginia, transcript in Family Letters Digital Archive, Thomas Jefferson Foundation, Inc., http://www.monticello.org/familyletters.
16. George Pierson to Albert Pierson, Nov. 2, 1825, Albert and Shirley Small Special Collections Library, University of Virginia.
17. "Minutes of the Faculty," June 18, 1825.
18. Ibid.
19. Ibid., Sept. 20, 1825.
20. Jefferson, *Writings*, 344.
21. "Minutes of the Faculty," Oct. 3, 1825.
22. Jefferson, *Writings*, 344.
23. Tutwiler, *Address*, 8.
24. Ibid., 9.
25. Ibid., 10.
26. Ibid.
27. Smith, *First Forty Years*, 229.
28. Tucker, *Life of Thomas Jefferson*, 2:481.
29. Wall, "Students and Student Life," 76.
30. Smith would go on to become a surgeon in the Confederate army. Bolling would become a circuit judge and a member of the Virginia legislature.
31. "Minutes of the Faculty," Oct. 5, 1825.
32. Martha Jefferson Randolph to Ellen W. Randolph Coolidge, Nov. 26, 1825, Ellen Wayles Randolph Coolidge Correspondence, University of Virginia, transcript in Family Letters Digital Archive, Thomas Jefferson Foundation, Inc., http://www.monticello.org/familyletters.
33. "Letters of Francis Walker Gilmer," *Tyler's Quarterly Magazine* 6 (1925): 197.
34. "Minutes of the Board of Visitors of the University of Virginia," Oct. 7, 1825.
35. Ibid., Mar. 4, 1825.

36. Ibid., Oct. 3, 1825.
37. Ibid.
38. Ibid.
39. Martha Randolph to Ellen Coolidge, Oct. 13, 1825, Ellen Wayles Randolph Coolidge Correspondence, University of Virginia, transcript in Family Letters Digital Archive, Thomas Jefferson Foundation, Inc., http://www.monticello.org/familyletters.

40. George Ticknor to James Madison, Mar. 29, 1825, Founders Early Access, University of Virginia Press, http://rotunda.upress.virginia.edu/founders/FOEA.html.
41. George Ticknor to James Madison, Nov. 21, 1825, American Founding Era Collection, University of Virginia Press, http://rotunda.upress.virginia.edu.

5. Tales of Horror

1. Edgar Allan Poe to John Allan, Sept. 21, 1826, University of Virginia Library, http://etext.lib.virginia.edu/services/courses/rbs/99/rbspoe99.html.
2. Dunglison, *Autobiographical Ana*, 23.
3. Madison to Jefferson, Jan. 15, 1823, in Madison, *Writings*, 114.
4. One can imagine the effect Poe's fantastic charcoal images would have on a visitor to the small dorm room. Poe must have stood on a chair or his bed, neck craned, to sketch the life-size image of Lord Byron on the ceiling. Did the university scrub the drawings from the walls after he left the school or are the elaborate figures still there under layers of paint applied over nearly two centuries?
5. Ronald Head, "Declension of George W. Blaettermann, First Professor of Modern Languages at the University of Virginia," *Virginia Cavalcade* 31 (1982): 187.
6. Ingram, *Edgar Allan Poe*, 38.
7. Poe, "Autobiographical Fragment" (manuscript), Poe Museum, Richmond, VA.

8. Edgar Allan Poe to John Allan, May 1826, University of Virginia Library, http://etext.lib.virginia.edu/services/courses/rbs/99/rbspoe99.html.
9. Ibid.
10. "Minutes of the Faculty," Feb. 26, 1826.
11. Ingram, *Edgar Allan Poe*, 36.
12. "Interview with Edmund Bacon, ca. 1860." In *22 Documents Concerning the Founding of the University of Virginia*, Electronic Text Center, University of Virginia Library, http://etext.lib.virginia.edu/toc/modeng/public/Jef14Gr.html.
13. Tucker, *Life of Thomas Jefferson*, 2:477.
14. Tutwiler, *Address*, 8.
15. Dunglison, *Autobiographical Ana*, 32.
16. Ibid.
17. Andrew K. Smith, "Account of Thomas Jefferson's Funeral," *Charlottesville Weekly Chronicle*, Oct. 15, 1875, transcript in Family Letters Digital Archive, Thomas Jefferson Foundation, Inc., http://www.monticello.org/familyletters. Jefferson's old nemesis and eventual

friend John Adams died at 6:20
p.m. the same day in Quincy,
Massachusetts.

18. "Resolution of the Faculty of the
University of Virginia," July 5, 1826.

19. Smith, "Account of Thomas
Jefferson's Funeral."

20. Dunglison, *Autobiographical Ana*, 32.

21. Tourists chipped off pieces of the
gravestone over the years. Congress
ordered a new obelisk in 1880.
Jefferson heirs gave the old one to
the University of Missouri.

22. Tutwiler, *Address*, 8.

23. "Minutes of the Faculty," Sept. 20,
1826.

6. Scholars amid Scofflaws

1. William D. Hoyt Jr., "Mr. Cabell,
Mr. Warden, and the University,
1823," *Virginia Magazine of History
and Biography* 49, no. 4 (1941): 352.

2. Cornelia Randolph to Ellen
Randolph Coolidge, Aug. 3, 1825,
Ellen Wayles Randolph Coolidge
Correspondence, University of
Virginia, transcript in Family Letters
Digital Archive, Thomas Jefferson
Foundation, Inc., http://www
.monticello.org/familyletters.

3. Bruce, *History of the University*,
2:22.

4. Ibid., 2:160.

5. Toynbee, "English Culture in
Virginia," 39.

6. Adams, *Thomas Jefferson and the
University*, 115.

7. Bruce, *History of the University*, 2:6.

8. Long, *Letters*, 23.

9. Cornelia Randolph to Ellen
Randolph Coolidge, Aug. 3, 1825,
Ellen Wayles Randolph Coolidge
Correspondence, University of
Virginia, transcript in Family Letters
Digital Archive, Thomas Jefferson
Foundation, Inc., http://www
.monticello.org/familyletters.

10. Cornelia Randolph to Ellen
Randolph Coolidge, Apr. 10, 1827,

Ellen Wayles Randolph Coolidge
Correspondence, University of
Virginia, transcript in Family Letters
Digital Archive, Thomas Jefferson
Foundation, Inc., http://www
.monticello.org/familyletters.

11. Bruce, *History of the University*,
2:33.

12. Cornelia Randolph to Ellen
Randolph Coolidge, Aug. 3, 1825,
Ellen Wayles Randolph Coolidge
Correspondence, University of
Virginia, transcript in Family Letters
Digital Archive, Thomas Jefferson
Foundation, Inc., http://www
.monticello.org/familyletters.

13. Joseph Coolidge to Nicholas P.
Trist, before Aug. 17, 1827, Nicholas
Philip Trist Papers, Library of
Congress, transcript in Family
Letters Digital Archive, Thomas
Jefferson Foundation, Inc., http://
www.monticello.org/familyletters.

14. Cornelia Randolph to Ellen
Randolph Coolidge, Aug. 3, 1825,
Ellen Wayles Randolph Coolidge
Correspondence, University of
Virginia, transcript in Family Letters
Digital Archive, Thomas Jefferson
Foundation, Inc., http://www
.monticello.org/familyletters.

15. Barringer and Garnett, *University of Virginia*, 347.
16. Dunglison, *Autobiographical Ana*, 55.
17. Of the original professors, five would be memorialized by the university. Bonnycastle, Dunglison, and Emmet have dormitory build-ings named after them. Entrance portals at Brown College on Monroe Hill are named for Long and Tucker.
18. "Minutes of the Board of Visitors," Oct. 2, 1826.
19. Ibid.

7. "A Most Villainous Compound"

1. "Journals of the Chairman," May 9, 1835.
2. Kierner, *Beyond the Household*, 147.
3. Ellis, Diary, May 10, 1835.
4. Ibid.
5. Wall, "Students and Student Life," 113.
6. Ellis, Diary, May 12, 1835.
7. "Journals of the Chairman," May 9, 1835.
8. "Minutes of the Board of Visitors," July 10, 1828.
9. Henderson would later serve in the nation's Electoral College.
10. "The Early Rising Law," *Collegian* 3 (June 1841): 291–292.
11. "Minutes of the Board of Visitors," Dec. 5, 1826.
12. Ibid.
13. Ibid.
14. Ibid.
15. "Minutes of the Faculty," Apr. 8, 1828.
16. Robert Lewis Dabney to his mother, Oct. 25, 1840, in Johnson, *Life and Letters of Robert Lewis Dabney*, 54. Dabney would later become a minister and professor at the Union Theological Seminary.
17. "Minutes of the Faculty," May 18, 1831.
18. Undated petition of students, University of Virginia Library.
19. Ellis, Diary, Mar. 12, 1835.
20. Bruce, *History of the University*, 2:231.
21. "Journals of the Chairman," Dec. 19, 1828.
22. Ibid.
23. "Minutes of the Faculty," June 26, 1828.
24. Ibid., June 28, 1828. Boyd later became a lawyer, legislator, and, ironically, a hotelkeeper.
25. "Minutes of the Faculty," Apr. 8, 1828.
26. Samuel Elias Mays, "Sketches from the Journal of a Confederate Soldier," *Tyler's Quarterly Magazine* 5 (1923): 109.

8. "Nervous Fever"

1. Smith, *Republic of Letters*, 3:1967.
2. Joseph Coolidge to Nicholas P. Trist, before Aug. 18, 1827, Nicholas Philip Trist Papers, transcript in Family Letters Digital Archive, Thomas Jefferson Foundation, Inc., http://www.monticello.org/familyletters.

3. Madison, *Writings*, 311.
4. "Minutes of the Faculty," May 18, 1827.
5. Ibid.
6. "For the Enquirer," *Richmond Enquirer*, Jan. 17, 1829.
7. "Minutes of the Faculty," Oct. 31, 1828.
8. Ibid.
9. Mary Randolph to Ellen Randolph Coolidge, Aug. 10, 1828, Ellen Wayles Randolph Coolidge Correspondence, University of Virginia, transcript in Family Letters Digital Archive, Thomas Jefferson Foundation, Inc., http://www.monticello.org/familyletters.
10. Ibid.
11. Ibid.
12. "Minutes of the Faculty," Feb. 26, 1829.
13. Ibid., Jan. 22, 1829.
14. "To the Editors of the Enquirer," *Richmond Enquirer*, Mar. 10, 1829.
15. "Journals of the Chairman," Jan. 23, 1829.
16. "Minutes of the Faculty," Jan. 22, 1829.
17. Ibid., Feb. 6, 1829.
18. Ibid.
19. Ibid.
20. Ibid., Feb. 10, 1829.
21. Ibid., Feb. 6, 1829.
22. Ibid.
23. Dunglison, *Autobiographical Ana*, 41.
24. "To the Editors of the Enquirer," *Richmond Enquirer*, Mar. 10, 1829.
25. Ibid.
26. Arthur Spicer Brockenbrough to John Cocke, Mar. 18, 1829. In 22 *Documents Concerning the Founding of the University of Virginia*, Electronic Text Center, University of Virginia Library, http://etext.lib.virginia.edu/toc/modeng/public/Jef14Gr.html.
27. Arthur Spicer Brockenbrough, "Subjects for Consideration," ca. 1828. In *Letters Concerning the Founding of the University of Virginia*, Electronic Text Center, University of Virginia Library, http://etext.lib.virginia.edu/toc/modeng/public/Jef13Gr.html.

9. Riot

1. "Journals of the Chairman," May 19, 1831.
2. Ibid.
3. Ibid.
4. "Minutes of the Board of Visitors," July 11, 1831.
5. "Journals of the Chairman," Oct. 17, 1831.
6. Ibid.
7. Ibid., Oct. 20, 1831.
8. Ibid., Feb. 15, 1832.
9. Ibid., Apr. 22, 1832.
10. "Minutes of the Board of Visitors," July 10, 1832.
11. "Journals of the Chairman," Nov. 6, 1832.
12. Opie would go on to become a Virginia legislator and to settle and die in Staunton, where he founded a newspaper dynasty.
13. "Journals of the Chairman," Dec. 8, 1832.

14. Ibid., Dec. 13, 1832.
15. Ibid.
16. Ibid., Feb. 3, 1833.
17. Ibid., Feb. 13, 1833.

18. Ibid., Feb. 17, 1833.
19. Ibid.
20. Ibid.

10. Diary of a College Boy

1. Ellis, Diary.
2. Among the women described by the girl-crazy Ellis were Miss Carter, Miss Mary, Miss Higgenbotham, the Misses Conroy, Miss Martha Coinors, Miss Gregory, Miss Bet, the Misses Conway, two Miss Browns, Miss Tucker, Miss Juliet Massie, Miss Mary McKenzie, Miss Ann Triplett, Miss Lizzy, Miss Parteaux, Miss Lane, Miss Ward, Miss Mary Ella Chapman, Miss Tutt, Miss Bonnycastle, Miss Walker, Miss Lucy Minor, the Misses Gordon, Miss Garrett, the Misses Winn, Miss Betsy Franklin, "the fair maid of Orange," Miss Emeline Gardner, Miss Hunton, Miss Ann Leiper, the three Miss Leipers, Miss Sampson, and Miss Willy Timberlake.
3. Ellis would go on to become president of the Richmond and Petersburg Railroad and a Confederate army colonel.

11. "Rebellion Rebellion!"

1. "Minutes of the Board of Visitors," Sept. 2, 1833.
2. "Minutes of the Faculty," Nov. 5, 1833.
3. Ibid., Nov. 6, 1833.
4. Patton, *Jefferson, Cabell, and the University*, 145.
5. Ibid., 146.
6. "Minutes of the Faculty," Feb. 24, 1834.
7. Ibid.
8. Ibid., Jan. 8, 1834.
9. Ibid., Feb. 28, 1834.
10. Ibid.
11. Wall, "Students and Student Life," 198.
12. "Minutes of the Faculty," July 4, 1833.
13. "Journals of the Chairman," Nov. 9, 1836.
14. Ibid.
15. Ibid., Nov. 10, 1836.
16. Patton, *Jefferson, Cabell, and the University*, 149.
17. Ibid.
18. Wall, "Students and Student Life," 197.
19. "Journals of the Chairman," Nov. 13, 1836.
20. A. G. Davis, "Exposition of the Proceedings of the Faculty of the University of Virginia in Relation to the Recent Disturbances at That Institution," 11, Library of Virginia.
21. "Journals of the Chairman," Nov. 14, 1836.
22. Ibid.
23. Patton, *Jefferson, Cabell, and the University*, 150.
24. Wall, "Students and Student Life," 203.

25. Ibid., 201.

26. "University of Virginia," repr. in *Richmond Enquirer*, Nov. 22, 1836.

27. Ibid.

28. "Journals of the Chairman," Nov. 22, 1836.

29. Patton, *Jefferson, Cabell, and the University*, 152–153.

12. "His Only Motive Was to Have a Little Fun"

The chapter title is taken from "Minutes of the Faculty," Nov. 16, 1837.

1. "Minutes of the Board of Visitors," Aug. 17, 1837.

2. "Minutes of the Faculty," Feb. 19, 1837.

3. Ibid.

4. Ibid.

5. "Report of the Committee of Schools and Colleges, in Relation to the Regulations of the University and Colleges of this State," *Virginia House of Delegates Journal*, 1837–1838.

6. "Minutes of the Faculty," Jan. 3, 1836.

7. Ibid., Feb. 1, 1837.

8. Ibid., Mar. 8, 1837.

9. Ibid., Apr. 12, 1837.

10. Ibid., Apr. 25, 1837.

11. Ibid., Mar. 31, 1838.

12. Rogers, *Life and Letters*, 1:157.

13. Ibid., 1:157–158.

14. Ibid., 1:158.

15. Ibid., 1:158–159.

16. Ibid., 1:158.

13. Caning, Whipping, Murder

1. "Minutes of the Faculty," Mar. 2, 1839.

2. Ibid.

3. Ibid.

4. Ibid.

5. Ibid.

6. "Journals of the Chairman," Feb. 25, 1839.

7. Ibid.

8. "Minutes of the Faculty," Mar. 2, 1839.

9. Ibid.

10. Ibid.

11. Ibid.

12. Ibid.

13. Ibid.

14. Ibid.

15. McAfee went on to become the state auditor of Mississippi and a quartermaster in the Confederate army; English would later die at the university; and Randolph would become the Confederate government's secretary of war.

16. "Journals of the Chairman," Mar. 19, 1839.

17. Rogers, *Life and Letters*, 1:162.

18. Ibid.

19. Ibid.

20. Johnson, *Life and Letters of Robert Lewis Dabney*, 58.

21. "University of Virginia," *Richmond Enquirer*, Dec. 1, 1840.

22. Johnson, *Life and Letters of Robert Lewis Dabney*, 58.

23. "Horrible Outrage," *Richmond Enquirer*, Nov. 13, 1840.

24. Ibid.

25. Johnson, *Life and Letters of Robert Lewis Dabney*, 57.
26. Ibid.

27. Rogers, *Life and Letters*, 1:176.
28. Ibid., 1:177.
29. Ibid.

14. Henry St. George Tucker and His "New" Old Strategy

1. Lipscomb, *Writings of Thomas Jefferson*, 15:455–456.
2. Thompson would go on to become editor of the *New York Evening Post*.
3. "Minutes of the Faculty," May 14, 1842.
4. Ibid., July 5, 1842.
5. Arthur Spicer Brockenbrough, "Subjects for Consideration," ca. 1828. In *Letters Concerning the Founding of the University of Virginia*, Electronic Text Center, University of Virginia Library, http://etext.lib.virginia.edu/toc/modeng/public/Jef13Gr.html.

6. "Minutes of the Faculty," Dec. 15, 1841.
7. Ibid.
8. Wall, "Students and Student Life," 249.
9. Bruce, *History of the University*, 3:56.
10. "Minutes of the Faculty," Mar. 2, 1841.
11. Ibid., May 22, 1841.
12. Rogers, *Life and Letters*, 1:206.
13. Wall, "Students and Student Life," 253.

15. Critical and Perilous Situation

1. "Minutes of the Faculty," Jan. 12, 1843.
2. Ibid., May 31, 1843.
3. Ibid., Nov. 30, 1844.
4. Ibid.
5. Rogers, *Life and Letters*, 1:399.
6. Ibid., 1:238.
7. Ibid., 1:241.
8. Ibid., 1:242.
9. Ibid., 1:410.
10. "Minutes of the Faculty," Apr. 23, 1845.
11. Bruce, *History of the University*, 3:114.
12. Rogers, *Life and Letters*, 1:247.
13. Tanner, "Joseph C. Cabell," 169.
14. Bruce, *History of the University*, 3:118.

15. Rogers, *Life and Letters*, 1:248.
16. "Riot at the University," *Richmond Whig*, Apr. 29, 1845.
17. "A True Account of the Late Disturbances at the University," *Richmond Whig*, May 2, 1845.
18. "The University," *Richmond Enquirer*, May 6, 1845.
19. "University of Va.," *Richmond Whig*, May 9, 1845.
20. "The University," *Richmond Whig*, May 14, 1845.
21. "The University," *Richmond Whig*, July 1, 1845.
22. "The Cause of Education," *Richmond Enquirer*, June 7, 1845.
23. "College in Richmond," *Richmond Whig*, June 20, 1845.

24. "The University," *Richmond Whig,* June 21, 1845.
25. "Some Virginia Lawyers of the Past and Present," *Green Bag* 10 (Mar. 1898): 121.
26. "Address of the Society of Alumni of the University of Virginia, Through Their Committee, to the People of Virginia," *Journal of the House of Delegates,* 1845–1846, document 15, 22.
27. Ibid., 16.
28. Ibid., 17.
29. Ibid., 19.
30. Ibid.
31. Ibid., 20.
32. Ibid.
33. "Annual Report of the Rector and Visitors of the University of Virginia, to the President and Directors of the Literary Fund for the Year Ending June 30, 1845," *Journal of the House of Delegates,* 1845–1846, document 15.
34. "Minutes of the Faculty," Jan. 24, 1846.
35. "Extracts from a Report of the Committee of Schools and Colleges, to the Legislature, Against the Expediency of Withdrawing the Annuity from the University," *Journal of the House of Delegates,* 1845–1846, document 15, 43.
36. Tanner, "Joseph C. Cabell," 169.

16. A New Kind of University

1. Jefferson and Cabell, *Early History of the University,* 332.
2. Adams, *Thomas Jefferson and the University,* 12.
3. Brubacher and Rudy, *Higher Education,* 361.
4. Ibid., 147.
5. Ibid.
6. Lipscomb, *Writings of Thomas Jefferson,* 15:303.

SELECTED BIBLIOGRAPHY

Adams, Herbert Baxter. *Thomas Jefferson and the University of Virginia*. Washington, DC: Government Printing Office, 1888.

Barringer, Paul, and James M. Garnett. *University of Virginia*. New York: Lewis, 1904.

Brant, Irving. *James Madison*. Vol. 6, *Commander in Chief, 1812–1836*. Indianapolis: Bobbs-Merrill, 1961.

Brodie, Fawn M. *Thomas Jefferson: An Intimate History*. New York: Bantam Books, 1985.

Brubacher, John S., and Willis Rudy. *Higher Education in Transition: A History of American Colleges and Universities*. New Brunswick, NJ: Transaction Publishers, 1997.

Bruce, Dickson D., Jr. *Violence and Culture in the Antebellum South*. Austin: University of Texas Press, 1979.

Bruce, Philip Alexander. *History of the University of Virginia, 1819–1919: The Lengthened Shadow of One Man*. 5 vols. New York: Macmillan, 1920.

Cabell, Nathaniel Francis, ed. *Early History of the University of Virginia as Contained in the Letters of Thomas Jefferson and Joseph C. Cabell*. Richmond: J. W. Randolph, 1856.

Cash, W. J. *The Mind of the South*. New York: Vintage Books, 1941.

Clinton, Catherine. *The Plantation Mistress: Woman's World in the Old South*. New York: Pantheon Books, 1982.

Coleman, Wim, and Pat Perrin. *The Amazing Erie Canal and How a Big Ditch Opened Up the West*. Berkeley Heights, NJ: Enslow, 2006.

Culbreth, David M. R. *The University of Virginia: Memories of Her Student-Life and Professors*. New York: Neale, 1908.

Dunglison, Robley. *The Autobiographical Ana of Robley Dunglison, M.D.* Transactions of the American Philosophical Society Held at Philadelphia for Promoting Useful Knowledge, vol. 53, part 8. Philadelphia: American Philosophical Society, 1963.

Dunn, Susan. *Dominion of Memories: Jefferson, Madison, and the Decline of Virginia*. New York: Basic Books, 2007.

Ellis, Charles, Jr. Diary. Albert and Shirley Small Special Collections Library, University of Virginia. Transcript published as "The Student Diary of Charles Ellis, Jr., March 10–June 25, 1835," ed. Ronald B. Head, *Magazine of Albemarle County History* 34–36 (1977–1978). All quotations are from the original manuscript.

Emerson, Ralph Waldo. *The Journals of Ralph Waldo Emerson*. Boston: Houghton Mifflin, 1910.

Fishwick, Marshall W. *Virginia: A New Look at the Old Dominion*. New York: Harper and Brothers, 1959.

Foley, John P., ed. *The Jeffersonian Cyclopedia: A Comprehensive Collection of the Views of Thomas Jefferson. . . .* New York: Funk and Wagnalls, 1900.

Ford, Lacy K., Jr. *Origins of Southern Radicalism: The South Carolina Upcountry, 1800–1860*. New York: Oxford University Press, 1988.

Freeman, Joanne B. *Affairs of Honor: National Politics in the New Republic*. New Haven, CT: Yale University Press, 2012.

Gispen, Kees, ed. *What Made the South Different? Essays and Comments*. Jackson: University Press of Mississippi, 1990.

Greenberg, Kenneth S. *Honor & Slavery: Lies, Duels, Noses, Masks, Dressing as a Woman, Gifts, Strangers, Humanitarianism, Death, Slave Rebellions, the Proslavery Argument, Baseball, Hunting, and Gambling in the Old South*. Princeton, NJ: Princeton University Press, 1996.

Hamilton, Alexander. *The Papers of Alexander Hamilton*. Edited by Harold C. Syrett and Jacob E. Cooke. Vol. 24. New York: Columbia University Press, 1976.

Hayes, Kevin J. *The Road to Monticello: The Life and Mind of Thomas Jefferson*. New York: Oxford University Press, 2008.

Howe, Daniel Walker. *What Hath God Wrought: The Transformation of America, 1815–1848*. New York: Oxford University Press, 2007.

Ingram, John Henry. *Edgar Allan Poe: His Life, Letters, and Opinions*. Vol. 3. London: Ward, Lock, Bowden, 1891.

Jefferson, Thomas. *Notes on Virginia*. In *The Works of Thomas Jefferson*. Edited by Paul Leicester Ford. Vol. 4. New York: G. P. Putnam, 1904–1905. Reprint, New York: Cosimo, 2009.

———. *Public and Private Papers*. New York: Vintage Books/Library of America, 1990.

———. *The Writings of Thomas Jefferson: Being His Autobiography, Correspondence, . . . and Other Writings*. 9 vols. New York: Derby and Jackson, 1859.

Jefferson, Thomas, and Joseph C. Cabell. *Early History of the University of Virginia, as Contained in the Letters of Thomas Jefferson and Joseph C. Cabell, hitherto Unpublished*. Richmond: J. W. Randolph, 1856.

Jefferson, Thomas, et al. *Report of the Commissioners Appointed to Fix the Scite [sic] of the University of Virginia*. Richmond: John Warrock, 1818.

Johnson, Thomas Cary. *The Life and Letters of Robert Lewis Dabney*. Richmond: Presbyterian Committee of Publication, 1903.

Kierner, Cynthia A. *Beyond the Household: Women's Place in the Early South, 1700–1835*. Ithaca, NY: Cornell University Press, 1998.

Larson, Edward J. *A Magnificent Catastrophe: The Tumultuous Election of 1800, America's First Presidential Campaign*. New York: Free Press, 2008.

Lipscomb, Andrew A., ed. *The Writings of Thomas Jefferson.* 20 vols. Washington: Thomas Jefferson Memorial Association, 1903–1904.

Long, George. *Letters of George Long.* Charlottesville: The Library, University of Virginia, 1917.

Luraghi, Raimondo. *The Rise and Fall of the Plantation South.* New York: New Viewpoints, 1978.

Madison, James. *The Writings of James Madison, 1819–1836.* Edited by Gaillard Hunt. Vol. 9. New York and London: G. P. Putnam's Sons, 1910.

Marsden, George M. *The Soul of the American University: From Protestant Establishment to Established Nonbelief.* New York: Oxford University Press, 1994.

Merwin, Henry Childs. *Thomas Jefferson.* Boston: Houghton Mifflin, 1901.

Miller, William Lee. *Arguing about Slavery: The Great Battle in the United States Congress.* New York: Alfred A. Knopf, 1996.

Minor, Franklin. *Address of the Society of Alumni of the University of Virginia, Through Their Committee, to the People of Virginia.* Charlottesville: Noel and Saunders, 1845.

Nisbett, Richard E., and Dov Cohen. *Culture of Honor: The Psychology of Violence in the South.* Boulder, CO: Westview, 1996.

Pace, Robert. *Halls of Honor: College Men in the Old South.* Baton Rouge: Louisiana State University, 2004.

Parton, James. *Life of Thomas Jefferson.* New York: Da Capo, 1971.

Patton, John S. *Jefferson, Cabell, and the University of Virginia.* New York: Neale, 1906.

Powell, J. H. *Bring Out Your Dead: The Great Plague of Yellow Fever in Philadelphia in 1793.* Philadelphia: University of Pennsylvania Press, 1949. Reprint, New York: Cosimo, 1985.

Rogers, William B. *Life and Letters of William Barton Rogers.* 2 vols. Boston: Houghton Mifflin, 1896.

Rosenfeld, Richard N. *American Aurora: A Democratic-Republican Returns; The Suppressed History of Our Nation's Beginnings and the Heroic Newspaper That Tried to Report It.* New York: St. Martin's, 1997.

Schulman, Gayle. "Slaves at the University of Virginia." Research project presented to the African American Genealogy Group of Charlottesville/Albemarle, 2005.

Shawen, Neil McDowell. "The Casting of a Lengthened Shadow: Thomas Jefferson's Role in Determining the Site for a State University in Virginia." Ph.D. diss., George Washington University, 1980.

Slosson, Edwin Emery. *Great American Universities.* New York: Macmillan, 1910.

Smith, James Morton, ed. *The Republic of Letters: The Correspondence between Thomas Jefferson and James Madison, 1776–1826.* Vol. 3. New York: W. W. Norton, 1995.

Smith, Margaret Bayard. *The First Forty Years of Washington Society. . . .* New York: C. Scribner's Sons, 1906.

Snow, Louis Franklin. *The College Curriculum in the United States.* New York: Teachers College, Columbia University, 1907.

Stampp, Kenneth M., ed. *The Causes of the Civil War.* Rev. ed. New York: Simon and Schuster, 1974.

Strupp, Jim. *Revolution Song: Thomas Jefferson's Legacy.* Summit, NJ: Ashland, 1992.

Tanner, Carol Minor. "Joseph C. Cabell, 1778–1856." Ph.D. diss., University of Virginia, 1948.

Ticknor, George. *Life, Letters, and Journals of George Ticknor.* Vol. 1. Boston: James R. Osgood, 1876.

Toynbee, Arnold. "English Culture in Virginia." *Johns Hopkins University Studies in Historic and Political Science,* Jan. 1889.

Tucker, George. *The Life of Thomas Jefferson, Third President of the United States.* 2 vols. Philadelphia: Carey, Lea, and Blanchard, 1837.

Tutwiler, Henry. *Address of H. Tutwiler, A.M., LL. D., of Alabama Before the Alumni Society of the University of Virginia, Thursday, June 29th, 1882.* Charlottesville: Charlottesville Chronicle Book and Job Office, 1882.

University of Virginia. "Journals of the Chairman of the Faculty, 1827–1864." Albert and Shirley Small Special Collections Library, University of Virginia.

Wall, Charles Coleman, Jr. "Students and Student Life at the University of Virginia, 1825–1861." Ph.D. diss., University of Virginia, 1978.

Williams, Jack. *Dueling in the Old South: Vignettes of Social History.* College Station: Texas A&M University Press, 1980.

Woods, Edgar. *Albemarle County in Virginia.* Charlottesville: Michie, 1901.

Wyatt-Brown, Bertram. *Honor and Violence in the Old South.* New York: Oxford University Press, 1986.

———. *The Shaping of Southern Culture: Honor, Grace, and War, 1760s–1880s.* Chapel Hill: University of North Carolina Press, 2001.

Index